T0330693

Innovation Driven Institutional Research

This is the third volume in the CARE-ing for Integral Development series. It continues to build on the previous two works, _Community Activation_ and _Awakening Integral Consciousness_, as well as preceding the fourth and final book, _Embodying Integral Development_. This book serves as a follow-up to the author's approach to integral research and development, economics and enterprise, contained within the Innovation and Transformation series, and as a focus for how to put all of this "CARE-fully" to work.

This third volume in the CARE quartet is perhaps the most crucial one, building on the organizational systems (see _Awakening Integral Consciousness_) that came before and turning from trans-cultural and transformational to trans-disciplinary, from integral reality and integral rhythm to integral realms, with a view ultimately to transpersonal, integral rounds. The author turns his attention to research and innovation, and then focuses in on enterprise and economics, management and leadership. As such, he introduces his _Inter-Institutional Genealogy_ in place of an "integral", yet still inhibiting, university.

In the process this book paves the way for a new kind of institutionalized, innovation driven social research, which, while rooted in a particular place, speaks to the world as a whole. Moreover, such a research-and-innovation institution has a fundamental role to play in the evolution of a specific community, building on what has come CARE-wise before.

Ronnie Lessem is the Co-Founder of Trans4m, Geneva. He has been a management educator and consultant in Africa, Asia, Europe and America and is the author of over thirty books on the development of self, business and society.

Transformation and Innovation
Series editors: Ronnie Lessem and Alexander Schieffer

This series on enterprise transformation and social innovation comprises a range of books informing practitioners, consultants, organization developers, development agents and academics how businesses and other organizations, as well as the discipline of economics itself, can and will have to be transformed. The series prepares the ground for viable twenty-first-century enterprises and a sustainable macroeconomic system. A new kind of R & D, involving social as well as technological innovation, needs to be supported by integrated and participative action research in the social sciences. Focusing on new, emerging kinds of public, social and sustainable entrepreneurship originating from all corners of the world and from different cultures, books in this series will help those operating at the interface between enterprise and society to mediate between the two and will help schools teaching management and economics to re-engage with their founding principles.

For a full list of titles in this series, please visit www.routledge.com/business/series/TANDI

Innovation Driven Institutional Research

Towards Integral Development

Ronnie Lessem

Routledge
Taylor & Francis Group

LONDON AND NEW YORK

First published 2017
by Routledge
2 Park Square, Milton Park, Abingdon, Oxon OX14 4RN

and by Routledge
711 Third Avenue, New York, NY 10017

Routledge is an imprint of the Taylor & Francis Group, an informa business

British Library Cataloguing in Publication Data
A catalogue record for this book is available from the British Library.

Library of Congress Cataloging in Publication Data
A catalog record for this book has been requested

ISBN: 978-1-138-74057-0 (hbk)
ISBN: 978-1-315-18339-8 (ebk)

Typeset in Times New Roman
by Swales & Willis, Exeter, Devon, UK

Contents

PART III
Navigation of institutionalized research 71

PART IV
Effect of institutionalized research 113

Figures

Tables

Prologue

Innovation driven institutionalized (social) research
Towards an inter-institutional genealogy

Introduction

Towards trans-disciplinary emancipation

In our previous two volumes on C_A_RE and CARE, we focused respectively on Community activation and the Awakening of integral consciousness, functionally, and on Creating a learning community, and on Actualizing innovation ecosystems, structurally. These in turn served as a prelude to innovation driven, institutionalized (social) Research, and to Recognizing inter-institutional genealogies, as we shall now see, functionally and structurally in turn. We thereby focused in particular, and respectively, on our integral *realities* (trans-cultural) and integral *rhythm* (transformational).

We turn in this third volume, as Trans4m, to what up to now has been ironically our "north-western" *Achilles heel*. I say "ironically" because so

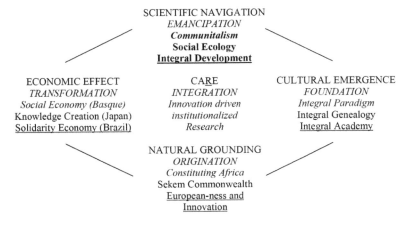

SCIENTIFIC NAVIGATION
EMANCIPATION
Communitalism
Social Ecology
Integral Development

ECONOMIC EFFECT
TRANSFORMATION
Social Economy (Basque)
Knowledge Creation (Japan)
Solidarity Economy (Brazil)

CARE
INTEGRATION
Innovation driven
institutionalized
Research

CULTURAL EMERGENCE
FOUNDATION
Integral Paradigm
Integral Genealogy
Integral Academy

NATURAL GROUNDING
ORIGINATION
Constituting Africa
Sekem Commonwealth
European-ness and
Innovation

Figure 0.1 Innovation driven institutionalized research.

much of our *integral* work has been focused on the "south" and "east" to counteract the dominance of the "north-west". This is particularly the case when it comes to research and innovation, generally, and to enterprise and economics, management and leadership, specifically. Yet, ultimately for us, the trajectory from local grounding (origination) and local–global emergence (foundation) to *newly global* navigation (emancipation), and then global–local effect (transformation), needs the "north-west" to build on the "rest" ("south" and "east"). As such, structurally, as we shall see, we introduce our *Inter-Institutional Genealogy* in place of even an "integral", yet still inhibiting, university.

The genius of the north-west, as such, lies in practical conceptualization and sustainable institutionalization, also combined with the trans-disciplinary, via our integral *realms*. So now we come on to this, which remains our unfinished business, at Trans4m in the latter half of 2016, though, with our proliferating emergent centres, most especially in Africa, but also in the Middle East and in Western as well as eastern Europe, we are beginning to get there! To that extent, then, this third volume in our CARE quartet is perhaps the most crucial one, indeed the source of our very emancipation, which we crucially align (see Chapter 8), building on the innovation ecosystem (see *Awakening Integral Consciousness*, Chapter 9) that came before, with what we term our *Inter-Institutional Genealogy*. As such, we turn, by way of emphasis, from trans-cultural and transformational to trans-disciplinary, from integral reality and integral rhythm to integral realms, with a view ultimately to transpersonal, integral rounds.

Relational, renewal and reasoned-realization trajectory

In pursuing a functional *CARE* and structural CARE overall, then, you are invited again to opt for one or other of the three paths, as you may have done previously for Community activation, and for Awakening integral consciousness, according to personal and situational choice. However, our inter-institutional genealogy, like our innovation-driven, institutionalized Research, and accompanying innovation ecosystem, needs, as we shall see, to draw on them all.

We now lay out each overall path in turn, each from Grounding to Effect. As such, we shall not be presenting this Prologue in chapter order (see Contents for this approach). We begin with *Constituting Africa*, as our original, relational, institutional research base, and indeed all-round polity, as our first stepping stone towards our *Inter-Institutional Genealogy*. This should come as no surprise, as genealogy requires us to go back to our roots. We start on the relational path.

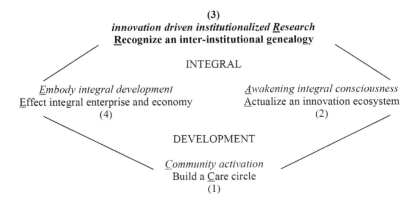

(3)
innovation driven institutionalized Research
Recognize an inter-institutional genealogy

INTEGRAL

Embody integral development   *Awakening integral consciousness*
Effect integral enterprise and economy   Actualize an innovation ecosystem
(4)   (2)

DEVELOPMENT

Community activation
Build a Care circle
(1)

Figure 0.2 CARE and CARE.

The relational path of innovation driven institutionalized research

Constituting Africa: relational path as southern grounding

For Afro-American twentieth-century historian Chancellor Williams (Lessem *et al.*, 2015) to begin with, as a faculty member of Howard University, an American research university that has played an important part in the civil rights movement, the African Constitution – as opposed to, say, the American or even today the South African one – is an original body of fundamental principles and practices drawn from the customary laws that governed Black African societies from the earliest times. Among the Blacks, then, original democratic institutions evolved and functioned in a socio-economic and political system that Western writers call "stateless societies". *Far from being a descriptive term for backward peoples, "primitive" in this context means "first", and "original"* – for us, *genealogical* grounding. Williams then spells out what *grounding-origins* have since been lost by Blacks. He focuses moreover, and in particular, on anthropology, as for him this is the leading social scientific discipline, taking us back to our roots, thereby underlying:

- *people as a first source of power;*
- *the family as a primary social, economic and political unit;*
- *land belonging to everyone, as God's gift to mankind, a scared heritage;*
- *age sets predetermining social, economic, political systems underlying education;*
- *religion as a way of thinking and living, not a creed or "articles of faith".*

Communitalism: relational path – emergent foundation

Communitalism today, spearheaded by Father Anselm Adodo (Lessem, 2016) as founder of *Paxherbals* in Nigeria, involves the generation of community-based knowledge through so-called *Pax Africana* in four guises. The *Learning Community*, represented by *EDEMCS*, is specifically formed to introduce knowledge sharing into the community. This is important to ensure that such a community, as in this case in Edo State, does not stagnate in past cultures and traditions, but is opened to the continuous creative and dynamic interaction between tradition and modernity, individual and community, as well as the indigenous and the exogenous. Promoting such is especially the role to be played by a contemporary *Developmental Sanctuary*, in this case the local–global *Benedictine Monastery.*

Moreover, an aligned *Research Academy*, in this case the *University of Ibadan's Institute for African Studies*, becomes a place of trans-disciplinary research, philosophy-in-action, where fundamental social research is undertaken, born out of society's needs and capacities, dynamically merged, in conjunction with applied research and ultimately innovation, finally through *Paxherbals* (the largest Nigerian producer of herbal medicines), as a *social* and medical *Laboratory*. It is a place where knowledge is translated into capabilities and capabilities are translated into knowledge. Education then takes its place fully embodied in the real life–*CARE*-ing world.

Social research paradigm: navigating relational institutional path

Taking on from where Chancellor Williams and Anselm Adodo leave off, as Trans4m Centre for Integral Development, our claim is that educational establishments tend to see research and education in invariably universalist terms (Lessem and Schieffer, 2010b). However, there is more, from the outset, to say "southern" *social* innovation than such a universalized one. *There is functionally, or at least should be, institutionalized social research and innovation, relationally lodged in a particular society,* as for example in countries and communities in Africa. After all, take the aftermath of the recent economic crisis, the plight of the European PIGS (Portugal, Italy, Greece, Spain), the advent of ISIS, the devastating war in Syria and indeed South Sudan today. All these "wicked problems" are in need of social – including the social sciences and the humanities – rather than merely technological innovation, invariably requiring an intimate appreciation (as above) of the grounding, and potential for emergence, in and of a particular society, before identifying a means of "navigating" and "effecting" research and development, alias social innovation. This is where our genealogy will come in.

So, genealogically and structurally and functionally, we have to start the social, including natural and cultural, process by acknowledging, developmentally and institutionally, the particular Grounds in which a society and community stands, while also, and subsequently, affirming that these local grounds never stand in global isolation (with the ever-decreasing exception of still isolated, indigenous peoples). *This blending of the local and the global is what we term Emergent development.* *However, and in addition, for social innovation to fully occur, such grounding and emergence needs to be consolidated, in terms of newly constituted institutional frameworks,* which we align with inter-institutional, "genealogical" Navigation. Finally, such organizational designs, or political constitutions, together with new conceptual frameworks, need to be put into Effect, in relation to a particular enterprise–community–society.

A social laboratory: effect of relational institutional research path

Finally, and effectively, such an overall CARE-ing approach, navigation-wise functionally and structurally, is magnificently amplified by the Mondragon Cooperatives in Spain, as the transformative relational effect of innovation driven, institutionalized social and technological research. Joxe Azurmendi, in his 1984 book *El Hombre Cooperative: Pensamiento de Jose Maria Arizmendiarrietta*, made an exhaustive analysis of the founder of Mondragon's writings and placed them in the political and economic context of his times. In these writings, located in the Spanish Basque country, early 1940s, the crisis of the times is seen by Azurmendi as a crisis of faith, viewed in terms of a specific system of Christian–humanist values. By about 1945–50, he was centring his attention on the broader social question. The nucleus of the crisis was no longer one of faith but that of property. After this, distinctly religious themes seem to disappear from his writings. Among secular authors that Azurmendi then drew upon were the leftist Catholic French social philosophers Jacques Maritain and Emmanuel Mounier, and the Brazilian emancipatory pedagogue Paulo Freire.

As such, and turning fundamental social research into transformative economic effect, he conceived of the Mondragon Cooperatives as a "business-based socio-economic initiative with deep roots in the Basque Country, created for and by people and inspired by the basic principles of our cooperative experience". Mondragon today, with its 100,000 cooperative members worldwide, operates on the basis of ten basic principles. These are *open admission, democratic organization, sovereignty of labour, the subordinate nature of capital, participatory management, payment solidarity, inter-cooperation, social transformation, universality and education.* Furthermore, as such, institutionally and genealogically, it is a veritable social and economic laboratory, duly sanctified through its Azurmendian origins, now with its own corporate university, rooted in the local Basque community. We next turn from the European "south", metaphorically if not geographically, to the Middle East.

The renewed path of innovation driven institutionalized research

Sekem Commonwealth: the renewal path as eastern grounding

As we then turn from a *relational* south towards an eastern path of *renewal*, so local grounding turns to local–global grounding and emergence, and the focus on Islamic religion and community specifically is aligned with a European society and philosophy generally. Locally, moreover, Sekem in Egypt has developed a sustainable agriculture, as an enterprise and a university (see Chapter 8) that resonates with Muslim teachings. Thereby *stewardship (Khalifa) implies social equality and dignity of all human beings regardless of skin colour and social status – a cardinal element of the Islamic faith.* Secondly, resources are a trust (*amanah*), provided by Allah, whereby the human being is not the primary owner, but is just a trustee (*amin*).

Locally–globally also, on this path of individual, organizational and societal renewal, the founder of Sekem, Dr Ibrahim Abouleish (2005), a research scientist in his own right (though explicitly in the natural, not the social, sciences), true to his cross-cultural Egyptian heritage, was a student of European polymath Rudolf Steiner, from whom the notion of *commonwealth* is drawn, whereby, as per fellow anthroposophist and social activist Martin Large (2013) in England,

> The key is to remake society as a Common Wealth . . . . The more that the principle of freedom informs our culture and civil society, the more that equality informs the state sector with its human rights, entitlements and responsibilities and the more mutuality guides business and economic life, the healthier, wealthier, more just and more resilient will be our society. And the more we care for nature and earth, the more resilient and sustainable our planet.

While Egypt is struggling to emerge from the recent Arab Spring, some of us in Zimbabwe, against the odds, are struggling to rise like an African phoenix.

De-coloniality: renewed south-eastern emergent institutional path

The emerging question our research associates in Zimbabwe have addressed, on the path of emergent renewal, is, how may they respond as a country, as an industry, as communities, as organizations and as individuals to burning issues – notwithstanding their particular gifts and capacities – which have resulted in a greater part of the population sinking into abject poverty (Mamukawa *et al.*, 2014)? There are currently (as of 2016) few jobs for the children to take up; the granaries do not have enough stocks to feed the people; while the majority of companies have closed, those factories and companies still limping along have lost critical skills; and the family structure has been split, with one parent taking up a job in the Diaspora, to mention just a few of the challenges we faced. So where do Zimbabweans go from here, by way of our emancipatory navigation of innovation driven, institutionalized research, functionally, and institutional genealogy, structurally?

Such social research and innovation, whether in Zimbabwe or South Africa, *would need to be embodied in de-coloniality, replacing "I am because I have power" with "I am because we are"*, connecting spirit, rhythm and creativity, with such interactive linkages leading to new meaning, motif, ethos, mode, function, method and form. This gives direction to research, *ultimately leading to the ecological rethinking of leadership, knowledge and industry*. Problems are tackled contextually, drawing on alternative knowledge systems: *Ubuntu-Unhu-Botho (humane-ness), Denhe re Ruzivo (calabash of knowledge) and Chitubu cheraramiso mumabasa (industrial fountain)*. These systems complement each other, culminating in an African phoenix that rises. However, for all of this to become an emancipatory reality, the respective research institutions, laboratories and communities involved, combined with the range of disciplines encompassed, in the social sciences and humanities, would need to constitute a genealogical whole, all together engaged in a sanctified cause.

The integral university: the reasoned path's emergent foundation

For us, at Trans4m (Schieffer and Lessem, 2014), initially with a view to building up an Integral University, specifically then applied to Heliopolis University for Sustainable Development in Egypt, we lodge our *renewed* integral, would-be "university", in each element of *CARE*, functionally (see Figure 0.3 below), if not yet *CARE* structurally. At the same time, we have to recognize that such a fully fledged, integral university design will inevitably be inhibited, to some extent functionally and to a great extent structurally, by the university powers that be, that is both the accrediting

INTEGRAL REALM	ACADEMY/*CARE* TYPE
Southern *nature & community* Theme: restoring life in nature and community Core value: healthy and participatory co-existence	*Community academy:* *community activation* Main focus: community-based learning and development Key terms: context, community, care
Eastern *culture and spirituality* Theme: regenerating meaning via culture and spirituality Core value: balanced and peaceful co-evolution	*Developmental academy:* *awakening integral* *consciousness* Main focus: societal learning and consciousness raising Key terms: catalyzation, consciousness, conscientization
Northern science, systems and *technology* Theme: reframing knowledge via science, systems and technology Core value: open and transparent knowledge creation	*Research academy:* *innovation driven, institutionalized* *Research* Main focus: scholarship, research and knowledge creation Key terms: content, concepts, complexity
Western enterprise and economics Theme: rebuilding infrastructure and institutions via enterprise and economics Core value: equitable and sustainable livelihoods	*Academy* *of life: integral Embodiment* Main focus: capacity building and individual realization Key terms: capacity, co-creation, contribution

Figure 0.3 The integral university as a whole.

authorities and conventional faculty, which is why we have ultimately come up with our alternative, inter-institutional, genealogy.

Knowledge creating enterprise: transformative effect of renewal path

We now turn from university navigation to enterprise effect, still on the renewal path. In fact, for the Japanese organizational sociologists Nonaka and Takeuchi (1995), most organizations, including conventional universities that "teach" specific courses and "run" research programs, only have specific products and services (for universities, usually courses though sometimes research projects) in mind when formulating their strategy. Such discrete offerings have clear boundaries. In contrast, boundaries for knowledge, in a specifically *knowledge creating company*, are more obscure, helping to expand the organization's cultural, economic, technological and social scope, through what Nonaka and Takeuchi term processes of socialization (our Grounding), externalization (our Emergence), combination (our Navigation) and internalization (our Effect), as indeed, in our terms, a GENE-alogical knowledge spiral.

Therefore, the three key "enabling conditions" for them are:

- first, developing intentionally the organizational *capability to acquire, create, accumulate and exploit knowledge*;
- second, *building up autonomous individuals and groups*, setting their task boundaries by themselves to pursue the intention of the organization;
- third, providing knowledge workers with *a sense of crisis – as well as a lofty ideal* – as so-called "creative chaos" increases tension within the organization.

We now turn from the "southern" relational and "eastern" renewal paths to the "north-western" path to innovation driven, institutionalized research, as we shall see, of reasoned realization, and thereby first to Europe.

The path of reasoned realization in institutionalized research

The European trinity: reasoned path as north-western grounding

For a management research group of which I was part, commissioned by Germany's Roland Berger Foundation (Kalthoff *et al.*, 1996), in the 1990s, the European reasoned quest for realizing knowledge began in ancient Athens in the age of Socrates, albeit many would argue that ancient Athens in Europe drew in turn on ancient Egypt in Africa. It was Socrates, arguably then, who first steered the course of human inquiry towards things of the physical world rather than the gods and supernatural phenomena; it was the student of Socrates, Plato, who first elaborated a set of ideals that humanity could reach through art, science and design. In effect *truth, goodness and beauty were the three ideals that Plato viewed as the goals of a just society.*

The pursuit of these fundamentals has occupied European innovators in every sphere of thought, feeling and action ever since. *All research and innovation, then, following this trinity of beauty, goodness and truth in a European context, can be roughly divided into three types*: those who seek excellence through alternately aesthetic appeal (beauty), managerial innovations (goodness), or – most commonly recognized – scientific discovery or technological advancement (truth). *Reason, moreover as such, was inclusive of not only the pursuit of truth, but also goodness and beauty.* Universities, arguably, are functionally focused on the first; business corporations have arguably lost touch with the second; and artistic institutions focus purportedly on beauty. In Slovenia in fact, we have tried to bring those three elements together.

Integral Green Slovenia: reasoned path as north-western navigation

For its co-founder and coordinator, Slovenian government official Darja Piciga (Piciga *et al.*, 2016), our Citizens' Initiative on *Integral Green Slovenia* was a multidimensional, multilayered process to which a large number of people and institutions have contributed. An initial academic impulse in fact, in the beginning of 2012, came from *Professor Matjaž Mulej, a leading social scientific researcher in the fields of systems theory and social responsibility and a tireless promoter of social innovation in the Slovenian economy and society,* through the research institute he established, IRDO, for social responsibility. *At a conference on social responsibility at the time, the idea of Slovenia's development as a model of an integral, low carbon economy and society was presented.*

In the period between November 2012 and March 2013, policy planning processes, in which Darja Piciga participated as a senior expert at the Ministry of Agriculture and the Environment, led her to the conclusion that in such Slovenian policies there were already important facets of the theory developed by Lessem and Schieffer (2010a) of *Integral Economics* (such as corporate social responsibility, social entrepreneurship, green economy) on which they could build. Moreover, these were a further extension of the prior work of theirs (2010b) she had read on *Integral Research*. She also realized that these concepts built on ethical cores that Slovenia and Lessem/ Schieffer shared and *all served to promote self-sufficiency, a developmental economy, a social and a living economy*.

A crucial milestone on the path was the foundation of the Citizens' Initiative, prepared and signed by a group of more than twenty distinguished Slovenian experts, and widely communicated in April 2013. Thereafter, in 2014/2015, a leading agricultural college in Slovenia, *BC Naklo, adopted the CARE framework to underlying its own Community, Awareness raising, institutional Research and transformative Educational activities*. At the same time a multitude of public, private and civic enterprises joined forces. How might a more thoroughgoing institutional genealogy then work in practice, today, in Africa and the Middle East, in Europe and in the Far East, in academe as well as in industry?

Institutional genealogy: navigating the renewal path

For Trans4m (Lessem *et al.*, 2013), serving to recognize and release individual and collective GENE-ius, so as to *CARE* for a particular society, also following in French post-modern philosopher Michel Foucault's (Prado, 2000) genealogical (going back to origins), functional footseps, *an Inter-Institutional Genealogy*, altogether structurally, *consists of community, sanctuary, university and laboratory*. We are then seeking, in the process of institutionalizing our CARE, to realize this in the twenty-first century.

Indeed, historically, in the ninth century, Baghdad had followed in the footsteps of the great Alexandrian library in Egypt. *Its House of Wisdom, as a kind of Sanctuary, gathered a multicultural scholarly community* to translate all known "foreign wisdom" into Arabic. *Community at the same time exists to safeguard the purpose of each person within it and to awaken the memory of that purpose by recognizing the unique gifts each brings to the world.* Moreover, *early Universities,* from the twelfth century in Bologna and Paris, were not deliberately founded; they *simply coalesced spontaneously around networks of students and teachers,* as nodes at the thickest in these networks.

Six centuries thereafter, and as a predecessor to the modern research university, the seminar approach to *pedagogy, launched at the University of Göttingen in Germany, aimed to reshape the inner person,* not to fashion cookie-cutter gentlemen by drilling them, as was customary in the prestigious universities. Scholarship had finally replaced scripture as the ultimate source of human knowledge. Finally, in the nineteenth century, *Laboratory scientists, after learning to control nature within the four walls of their experimental domains, capitalized on their methods to change the way people lived in homes, neighbourhoods, even whole countries.* Finally we turn to Brazil.

The solidary economy: Brazil's reasoned path of navigating research

In Brazil hitherto, it was a leading research institute that also played a seminal role in its contemporary, democratic development towards a solidary economy, and as such played a major part in effecting social, political and economic transformation, through innovation driven institutionalized research.

Four decades ago an academic sociologist, Fernando Cardoso (Lessem, 2015), first emerged as a significant player in the gradual process of political reopening that began in 1973. The Brazilian Democratic Movement (MDB) was the main political organization demanding the return of democracy in the 1970s. *A Brazilian Research Centre for Analysis and Planning task force played a distinguished supporting role in the MDB struggle. Its very success in creating space to study alternative views about Brazilian society turned this innovative research centre and its leaders into actors in the democratic movement.*

Embedded in this, *the Cardosian worldview accepted the leading economic role of the market, while maintaining that it does not address all needs, creates problems of its own and tends to dissolve human solidarity.* So the state, through public alongside private enterprise, needed to play a fundamental role in reducing inequality, poverty and other social problems. In Cardoso's inaugural speech as President, in 1995, he said the development of a country is not measured by what it produces. *True development is measured by the quality of attention the country gives to its people and its culture.* In a world of instantaneous global communication where people fragment and specialize, *cultural identity is rooted in nations.* Brazilians, he said, are people of great communal and cultural heterogeneity, born from a combination of occidental Portuguese tradition with African and indigenous Indian traditions. *The collective support for the country is moved, moreover, by sentiment, and this sentiment has a name: solidarity.*

Arguably, such a sentiment formed the sanctified backdrop with which communities and enterprises alike, set alongside the kind of academic research institute that initially spearheaded such a solidary economy, could align themselves. Of late, however, much of such structurally laden CARE represented by a would-be institutional genealogy seems to have fallen apart. We now turn to our opening chapter on *Constituting the South*, setting the communal stage for innovation driven, institutionalized research to follow.

References

Abouleish, I. (2005) *Sekem: A Sustainable Community in the Egyptian Desert.* Edinburgh: Floris Books.

Azurmendi, J. (1984) *El Hombre Cooperative: Pensamiento de Jose Maria Arizmendiarrieta.* Mondragon: Consejo General de la MCC.

Kalthoff, O. *et al.* (1996) *The Light and the Shadow: Breakthroughs in European Innovation.* Oxford: Capstone.

Large, M. (2013) *Commonwealth: For a Free, Equal, Mutual and Sustainable Society.* Stroud: Hawthorne Press.

Lessem, R. (2015) *Integral Advantage: Revisiting Emerging Markets and Societies.* Abingdon: Routledge.

Lessem, R. (2016) *The Integrators: Beyond Leadership, Knowledge and Value Creation.* Abingdon: Routledge.

Lessem, R. and Schieffer, A. (2010a) *Integral Economics: Releasing the Economic Genius of Your Society.* Abingdon: Routledge.

Lessem, R. and Schieffer, A. (2010b) *Integral Research and Innovation: Transforming Enterprise and Society.* Abingdon: Routledge.

Lessem, R., Schieffer, A., Rima, S. and Tong, J. (2013) *Integral Dynamics: Cultural Dynamics, Political Economy and the Future of the University.* Abingdon: Routledge.

Lessem, R., Abouleish, I., Pogacnik, M. and Herman, L. (2015) *Integral Polity: Aligning Nature, Culture, Society and Economy.* Abingdon: Routledge.

Mamukawa, E., Lessem, R., and Schieffer, A. (2014) *Integral Zimbabwe: An African Phoenix Rising.* Abingdon: Routledge.

Nonaka, I. and Takeuchi, H. (1995) *The Knowledge Creating Company.* Oxford: Oxford University Press.

Piciga, D., Schieffer, A. and Lessem, R. (2016) *Integral Green Slovenia: Toward a Knowledge and Value Based Society and Economy at the Heart of Europe.* Abingdon: Routledge.

Prado, C. (2000) *Starting with Foucault: An Introduction to Genealogy. Second Edition.* Boulder, CO: Westview Press.

Schieffer, A. and Lessem, R. (2014) *Integral Development: Realizing the Transformative Potential of Individuals, Organizations and Societies.* Abingdon: Routledge.

Part I

Grounding of institutionalized research

1 Constituting the South

A historical perspective on institutionalized research

Summary of chapter:

1 anthropologically constituting original democracy in stateless societies;
2 interactive linkages connected in temporary genealogies continually reforming;
3 governance through cooperatively self-governing mutual consensus;
4 evolving male and female age sets as social, economic and political systems;
5 ultimately grounding science in anthropology not physics.

Introduction: relational path to grounding institutionalized research

Constitution, commonwealth, creation

In *Grounding* your innovation-driven *Institutionalization* of research, you and we start in the *relational* "south", not as conventionally in the European and American "north-west". As such our genealogical starting point in Chapter 1, functionally if not also structurally, not unnaturally, is with the birthplace of humankind, *Constituting* Africa in the "south", politically, legally and educationally, thereby trans-disciplinary-wise as per now our *integral realms*.

As such we stand, in this southern, relational and functional guise, on the giant research shoulders of the late African–American historian Chancellor Williams, constituting, or indeed reconstituting Africa. Moreover, Williams was a key faculty member of the history department of Howard University in the US, which has historically and structurally played a major part in advancing America's civil rights movement. Williams was born in 1893 in South Carolina, the son of an ex-slave and a mother who was a domestic. By 1950, having become an academic and thereby taught American, European and Arabic history, Williams considered himself prepared, now well into his midlife, for intense research on African social and political origins. Over the next 17 years he conducted field studies in 25 different African countries, in 105 different languages. The first fruits of these studies comprised the publication, in 1971, of *The Destruction of Black Civilization* (Williams, 1987), discussing the period from 4500 BC to AD 2000.

Having spent all those years undertaking fundamental social research for the book, most especially focused on Ghana, his personal country of origin, and having mortgaged his home to fund this, Williams' intention to produce a three-volume work was foreshortened by the fact that he went blind. Nevertheless, *The Rebirth of African Civilization* (Williams, 1993) was subsequently published. Williams died in 1992 and his books contain his ongoing legacy. This exists in four parts (see Lessem *et al.*, 2014):

- first, exploring "*the destruction of black civilization*", over the millennia;
- second, a review of the distinctively original, continent-wide "African Constitution", the *communitarian* form of African governance that, unbeknown to most, preceded the representative democracy – more usually attributed to the Greeks – now spreading across the globe;
- third, a depiction of *how such communal origins were subsequently in most instances dissipated*, or destroyed, but in some distinctive cases further evolved, at least to a point; and
- finally, discussing *how Black people should face up to their destiny, at the crossroads*, with a view to their future navigation, and thereby institutionalization, drawing research-wise upon a reconstructed anthropology-cum-polity.

Black history: destruction and resurrection of civilization

The main features of the longstanding history, or indeed genealogy, of the Black Africans, overall then for Chancellor Williams, were depicted by him as,

- *building* an advanced system of life, then having it *destroyed*;
- *building* again, but being destroyed again, migrating and building somewhere else, only to be sought out *and destroyed again*;
- moving, moving, *always moving* and rebuilding;
- *internal strife* increasing as *external threats* increased;
- an *every-man-for-himself* philosophy *replacing* that of *eternal brotherhood*;
- through it all, *new states continually forming*, renewing;

- *their lost civilization,* their written languages, their lost arts and sciences, having come down *in outline form generation to generation,* for us underlying African gene-ius;
- finally, Africans were still *rebuilding their own civilization when that of Asia and Europe was imposed.*

Towards an original African Constitution

Having sketched out these main historical characteristics of the Blacks, Williams then turned specifically to what he termed the original African Constitution, including the birth of its political democracy, legal judiciary, human and social rights, and approach to education. This would seem for us to be his seminal "southern" contribution to our work here, through his trans-disciplinary, innovation driven institutional research, as member of a longstanding group of African–American scholars at Howard University's history department in the US.

African Constitution: democracy, judiciary, human rights, education

Origin of African democracy and polity: stateless societies

For Williams, *the African Constitution is a body of fundamental theories, principles and practices drawn from the customary laws that governed Black African societies from the earliest times.* The first task for him was to divorce traditional African institutions from those influenced by later Asian and European incursions; to determine what is truly African in origin. Another task was to determine whether an institution called "African" was in fact

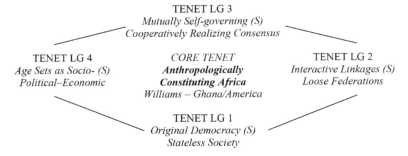

Figure 1.1 Relational institutional research: grounding tenets.

African in the sense of being universal among the Blacks, a continent-wide institution, as opposed to something particular to a specific tribe.

Williams' foregoing observations, based on his extensive research, also standing on the shoulders of scholarly others at Howard University in America, suggest that the constitution of any people or nation, written or unwritten, derives from its customary rules of life; and that *what we now call "democracy" was generally the earliest system among various peoples throughout the ancient world.* What was a relatively new development, then, was absolute monarchy.

Among the Blacks, democratic institutions evolved and functioned in a "primitive" socio-economic and political system that Western writers call "stateless societies". Far from being just a descriptive term for backward peoples, *"primitive" in this context means "first", and "original";* for us, original genealogical "grounding". The amazing thing was, for Williams, the uniformity of this Black approach, continent wide. It involved, then, a network of kinsmen, all of whom descended from the same ancestor or related ancestors. The ancestor from whom they claimed descent, moreover, was always "great", because of some outstanding accomplishments. Each generation of poets and storytellers, reviewed through Williams' study of African humanities, magnified the ancestor's image. Their nation, as such, became one big brotherhood.

Accordingly, instead of first attempting to conquer and annex other peoples by force, Blacks would approach independent states and seek to demonstrate from oral history that all of them were segments of a shared lineage. All were brothers. *This lineage, prior to the rise of kingdoms in*

Table 1.1 Constituting Africa

Innovation driven institutionalized research: relational path Grounding knowledge socio-politically contributes to African Constitution building

- *Communal attributes*: Grounding – **Constituting Africa**, Sekem Commonwealth, European Trinity; Emergence – social research paradigm, social ecology, integral development; Navigation – communitalism, integral university, reinventing knowledge; Effect – social economy, knowledge creation, solidarity economy.
- *Integrator role*: researcher and innovator, e.g. Chancellor Williams.
- *Research function*: scholarship, research and knowledge creation leading to **constitutional development**.
- *Navigating knowledge creation*: **anthropologically** constituting **original democracy** *in stateless societies*; interactive linkages connected in **temporary federations**, as per institutional genealogies that are continually reforming; problems are tackled through **self-governing** attempts at **realizing consensus**; at best, systematically undertaken, innovation driven, serving to follow **evolving male and female age sets as social, economic and political systems.**

particular, was the governing and organizing force, promoted by community consensus. Kinship found expression in trade and in temporary confedera-tions. In the "tribal war" that ensued, the main objective was to frighten away the adversary rather than to kill. This raises the issue of whether we have in fact become more "civilized" today. Have we not substituted the trappings of civilization, Williams maintains, that is, our triumphs in science, technology and the computer "revolution", for civilizational woes? He then turns to the typical African judicial system.

Earliest African judiciary: government by the people

In the chiefless African state (stateless society), then, the function of the elders was wholly advisory. For this reason, they rarely met as a council, except when called by the Senior Elder to an emergency meeting. Matters involv-ing the members of the same family or clan would be settled by the family council, each family or clan having its own elder. Conflicts between families or clans could be brought before any mutually acceptable elder for settlement. The elder's judgement was not binding, and if there was any remaining dis-pute additional elders could be called upon to exercise judgement. Moreover, the community as a whole was represented in the ever-present crowd, at such hearings, and its members would indicate their approval or otherwise.

The constitutional theory and principle here is especially significant, for Williams, because of the important form it took in all African societies in every part of the continent as societies evolved from those without chiefs to centralized states under chiefs, kings and emperors. In this continent-wide constitutional development, the chief or king became the mouthpiece of the people and the instrument for carrying out their will. The people still had no ruler in the Asian or European sense. In the chiefless societies, however, the elders were the overseers of land distribution to families. Finally, *nothing contributed more to the efficiency and success of self-government without governors than the system wherein each age grade was responsible for the conduct of its members* (see detailed description of this below) and the fact that before any misconduct could reach one's age-grade council it was han-dled by the family council. Stated another way, each family policed itself, each age group policed itself, so there was little the community as a whole needed to do. For Williams (1993),

> *It was therefore in the societies without chiefs or kings where African democracy was born and where the concept that the people are sover-eign was naturally breathing. Theirs was in fact a government of the people. That this kind of government did "pass from the earth" is what we call "modern progress".*

So what does this all imply, for Williams, for the fundamental rights of the African people, as per their original, democratic constitution?

The fundamental rights of the African people

Williams, in fact at this point, spells out in more detail (1993), spanning as such anthropology, sociology, political science, religious and educational studies, what has since been lost by Blacks, starting with what were their fundamental rights:

- the *people are the first and final source of power*;
- the *rights of the community are superior to those of any individual*;
- elders, *chiefs*, kings as leaders, *not rulers, exercise the will of the people*;
- *the family is* recognized as *the primary social, economic and political unit*;
- *the land belongs to no one* – it is God's gift to mankind, a scared heritage;
- *each family has a free right to the land*, as a means to make a living;
- *"royalty" means royal worth* – highest in character, wisdom and justice;
- *age sets are social, economic and political systems* underlying education, roles and responsibilities, division of labour and rights of passage;
- *the community is to be conceived as one party*, opposition being conducted by leaders of factions formed by different age groups, with debates being held until there is *consensus*;
- *African religion is a way of thinking and living*, not a creed or "articles of faith", reflected in all institutions, whereby politically the High Priest who presents the prayers of the people and their ancestors is key – and socially, the "rites of passage" via songs and dances are important.

Suffice to say, the steady weakening of lineage ties and the spirit of unity was also a weakening of the sense of brotherhood and unity among Blacks. *Lineage, then, was the most powerful and effective force for unity and stability in early Africa, and this was so true that a state could be self-governing without the need for any individual ruler, chief or king.* Everyone was a lawyer because just about everyone knew the customary laws. The age grade or age set, moreover, was the specific organizational structure through which the society governed. There was seniority in each grade according to age and intelligence. The age set, then, underpinned the whole African approach to education, and arguably to communal if not also institutionalized (in traditional guise) research and development, as we shall see. It seems that this approach to education and research has been totally by-passed today, rather than being renewed. No wonder African students, if not also staff, are so often on strike!

Williams (1993) then turns specifically, and most originally as well as for us in Foucault's terms genealogically, to African "age sets".

Original African education constituted in age sets

Age group A: primary childhood and education, 6–12, games and play

Each age set, traditionally then, had its own social, economic and political role. The children's set, to begin with, covered, in trans-disciplinary guise, the years of games and play. *Primary education, and indeed research, included storytelling, mental arithmetic, community songs and dances, learning the names of various birds and animals,* the identification of poisonous snakes, local plants and trees, and how to run and climb swiftly when pursued by dangerous animals.

Age group B: secondary teenage-hood and education, 13 to 18, life skills

The next grade set above childhood involved teenage-hood (these periods varied of course among different societies). Now both education and responsibilities were stepped up, becoming more complex and extensive. The youth's entire future depended upon their performance, research and education wise, at this level. *The boy was now required to learn his extended family history and that of the society, including also the geography of the region, names of neighbouring states and the nature of the relations with them.* He had to learn the handling of weapons, hunting as a skilled art, rapid calculation, clearing the bush for planting, the nature of soils and which grow best, military tactics, the care and breeding of cattle, bartering tactics, the rules of good manners at home and abroad, the division of the sexes, and competitive sports.

The girl's age group differed from that of the boys. While they had the same intellectual education as the boys – history, geography, rapid calculation, poetry, music and dance – *the education and training in childcare, housekeeping, gardening, cooking and marketing, as well as social relations* was distinct to their group.

Age group C: tertiary personhood/education, 19–28, agriculture/industry

At the next stage, *male members led in hunting, community construction, preparing the fields for planting, forming the various industrial craft guilds* (secret societies, each of which guarded the processes of the art), protecting the far-ranging grazing cattle, the upkeep of roads and paths between villages, and policing where necessary.

The young women were generally responsible for planting and care of the farms, the operations of the markets (hence the stress on mental arithmetic in their earlier education), *visiting and care of the sick and aged, formation of women's societies* (the media for women's very real political influence), *and overall responsibility for the home.*

Age group D and E: post-experience eligibility for election, 29–40 and onwards

There was not much difference, thereafter, between age groups C and D, for both men and women – whose constitutional rights were inseparable. *At the age of 36, then, if suitably qualified, men and women were eligible for election to the most highly honored body of society, the Council of Elders*, most especially reserved, through, for age set E, that is, from 40 years onwards.

So much for the profoundly original African local grounding, as a whole, educationally, culturally, politically, economically. What, then, is the contemporary implication of such constituting of Africa, today, generally, and for the grounding of our "southern" innovation driven, institutionalized research, functionally, and our institutional genealogy, structurally, specifically?

Conclusion: reconstituting Africa

Cooperative programs and renewal of age sets

The first line of action, Williams says, research and innovation wise, *should centre around the study and development of nationwide, people-involved, self-help cooperative programs, village by village, town by town and block by block* that draw upon, and serve to renew, African democracy, judiciary, human rights and "education sets". Of course he regrettably fails to institutionalize these.

First, each community, then, would do its own development planning, the government's principal role being to provide advisors, technical assistance and loans when and where these are needed. Economically speaking, for people with little or no money, barter and exchange would be the first steps towards economic salvation, as the bases for capital formation. Increased food production should be seen as beneficial for both wealth and health. Plans should be made, by mutual agreement, in each region to produce goods needed but not produced in the other region.

The second great task of government calls for furthering the home front of economic development by aggressively working for economic unity on a scale never before attempted, across Africa as a whole. Every one of the great Black nations that Williams studied rose as the result of a wealth-producing system that enabled it to achieve set goals. The crying need throughout the African world thereafter, however, is dedicated leaders (again, no institutionalization), not just office-holding bureaucrats, but men and women leaders who will be more and more in the field among the people, and less and less preoccupied with office work. These will be people on a mission, as was the case historically for a Bernard Ouedraogo in Burkina Faso (see our previous work on *Community Activation for Integral Development*), and currently for Father Anselm Adodo of Paxherbals in Nigeria, to improve the lives of people, rather than enriching themselves. Sadly, thus far, Williams leaves out the structural dimension.

Constitution building locally anew

Some of the Black people of the world, he says, have today come to destiny's crossroads. And there is, for Williams, a terrible crisis of functional leadership (we would add, structural institutionalization). *The great difficulty is that Black leaders, unlike for example the Jews, do not know what their own heritage is*, for us their genealogy. They are almost wholly ignorant, he says, of their own cultural and institutional source from which independent, original thinking springs and progress is inspired, coupled with the ability to resurrect and renew these. They wish rather to draw on the Caucasian heritage and become identified with it.

To be equal to the required task such Black leaders need to stand on their own individual, communal and institutional feet. Instead, Williams goes on to say, the immediate trouble confronting the Blacks is that so many millions of them have been made wholly dependent on – or indeed have reacted against – the white, if not also now the yellow, race for so many generations that they have become mentally lazy. So where do we go from here?

The greatest discovery of our age: anthropology not physics

In fact, and perhaps most importantly for us in terms of the *integral realms* that we significantly feature here, Williams maintains, *one of the greatest discoveries of this age* has been made in the field of anthropology, not physics. It is *the discovery that in the rush from primitive life man actually left behind some of the more fundamental elements needed for a truly civilized life. Chief among these was – and of course is – the original trans-disciplinary sense of democracy, judiciary, human rights and set education.*

This is why Africa in the "south" is very important now. It can profit if it sees the precipice towards which we are drifting, and takes the opposite course in an effort to build a different kind of society in a spiritual foundation, for us functionally lodged in a duly and newly institutionalized, anthropologically informed, social research (*CARE*), and also structurally reconfigured in inter-institutional genealogical terms (CA<u>RE</u>), as we have set out in Chapter 9, leading purposefully from community to laboratory, via academy and sanctuary.

The tasks Africa now faces, he says overall, will test the genius of the Black race. If we fail to accept this challenge, Williams asserts, at this critical turning point, we shall have proved ourselves unworthy of having any descendants, and our very names should be forgotten by them. Africa needs to return to its origins, its original African Constitution (grounding), in democracy, judiciary, human rights and education wise, altogether, and to then integrally renew (emergence) institutionalized research (navigation) and rebuild (effecting) it. In the process, for us, this will serve to innovatively develop, newly institutionalized, social research.

Community activation, awaken consciousness, institutional research

In summing up, then, Williams proclaims that his immediate concern lay in awakening African people who, after centuries of primitive life, have almost suddenly resolved to come abreast with the rest of mankind. But since the African people are just a part of the human family, and Africa is just a part of the world that, in spite of all the opposing forces, is becoming more closely knit, he has viewed it in a universal setting. He has then attempted to take the approach of an institutionalized (Howard University) researcher and a stranger from another planet who has found it necessary to study first the history of mankind and the character of the civilization of which Africa is emerging to become a part.

Indeed, preaching about the need for an "African Renaissance", and all such highly edifying discussion, he concludes, is idle unless it is followed up with a program of research-and-action that starts from the community, embodies institution building and knowledge creation, and what we term innovation driven institutionalized research. This involves, in conclusion for Williams, *anthropologically constituting original democracy in stateless societies; interactive linkages connected in temporary federations, as per institutional genealogies, continually reforming; governance through cooperatively self-governing mutual consensus; evolving male and female age sets as social, economic and political systems; ultimately grounding science in anthropology, not physics.*

We now turn, with a further view towards institutional research, and genealogy moving from the *relational* to the *renewal* path, from "southern" African Constitution to "eastern" Sekem Commonwealth, from Africa to the Middle East, albeit still connected to the South, in Egypt.

References

Lessem, R., Abouleish, I., Pogagnik, M. and Herman, L. (2014) *Integral Polity: Aligning Nature, Culture, Society and Economy*. Abingdon: Routledge.

Williams, C. (1987) *The Destruction of Black Civilization*. Chicago, IL: Third World Press.

Williams, C. (1993) *The Rebirth of African Civilization*. Chicago, IL: Third World Press.

2 Sekem Commonwealth

A commonwealth perspective on institutionalized research

Summary of chapter:

1 grounding and origination in the renewal and reinterpretation of Islam;
2 emergent foundation lodged in the fusion between the occident (anthroposophy) and the orient (Islam);
3 emancipatory navigation through anthroposophical approach to natural, cultural, political and economic systems;
4 transformatively effecting the reclamation of the desert;
5 thereby pursuing, via enterprise and academe, sustainable development.

Introduction: grounding renewed institutionalized research

A commonwealth integrator

We now turn, by way of further institutional research and genealogical grounding, in this next chapter to "eastern" *renewal* research wise. As such, we turn from Africa towards both Asia and Europe, via Egypt as the ancient, trans-cultural cross-roads of civilization. Moreover, the founder of Sekem in Egypt, on whose unfolding narrative and definitively evolving enterprise we shall be focusing here, Ibrahim Abouleish, was a student of Rudolf Steiner's trans-disciplinary anthroposophy. In fact it is from Steiner that the notion of a *commonwealth* has been drawn. Thereby for the UK's social activist Martin Large (2013), as a fellow anthroposophist and community economic developer:

> *The key is to remake society as a Common Wealth . . . . The more that the principle of freedom informs our culture and civil society, the more that equality informs the state sector with its human rights, entitlements and*

responsibilities and the more mutuality guides business and economic life, the healthier, wealthier, more just and more resilient will be our society. And the more we care for nature and earth, the more resilient and sustainable our planet.

As we can see, then, such a commonwealth spans the integral realms of culture, economy and polity, if not also ecology. For Maulana Karenga (2005), Chair of African Studies at California State University, as such, the ancient ideal of Maat, a keynote of that Egyptian society in which Sekem is today lodged, was *bringing about rightness in and of the world, that is giving rightful attention to self, society and the world as an interrelated order.* The ongoing quest, then, is to maintain, renew, repair and enhance this order as self-conscious creators and bringers of the good in the world in a process and practice called *serudj ta* – restoring, repairing and renewing the world, now locally and globally.

This is the role, for us, to be played by innovation driven, institutionalized research, functionally and dynamically, and by a stabilizing inter-institutional genealogy (see Chapter 9) structurally.

A vision of a sustainable community in the Egyptian desert

We draw then substantively, in this chapter, from the book of Ibrahim Abouleish, as the founder of Sekem, on *Sekem: A Sustainable Community in the Egyptian Desert*, and indeed the many years with which we have been working with him and the Sekem Group – now also Heliopolis University, as we shall see (Chapter 8) – over the course of the last decade.

Ibrahim Abouleish (2005), then, was born into a typical, though well-off, extended family in Egypt, with homes in both the city and countryside.

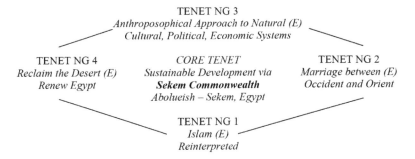

TENET NG 3
Anthroposophical Approach to Natural (E)
Cultural, Political, Economic Systems

TENET NG 4
Reclaim the Desert (E)
Renew Egypt

CORE TENET
Sustainable Development via
Sekem Commonwealth
Abolueish – Sekem, Egypt

TENET NG 2
Marriage between (E)
Occident and Orient

TENET NG 1
Islam (E)
Reinterpreted

Figure 2.1 Institutional research renewal: grounding tenets.

My grandfather listened to all my childlike questions and found comprehensive answers for me, which were deeply satisfying. He sat down beside the bright white flower with the dancing butterfly, and took me on his knee. I leaned back against him, enjoying his gentleness. The butterfly opened its colourful wings, and flew from the white blossom up into the sky. We both followed its flight for a long time.

Abouleish's childhood dream

Ibrahim's approach to education, given all that had come in his life before, inwardly and outwardly, was very different from that of his fellow students. He felt reminded, in revisiting his societal origins, of the golden era of Islam and the flourishing culture in Egypt, and this feeling never left him, originating, as it were, in his childhood, and returning to his consciousness, as we shall see, as he embarked on his university studies, inadvertently to start with perhaps, to ultimately pursue his childhood dream (2005).

I carry a vision deep within myself: in the midst of sand and desert I see myself standing as a well drawing water. Carefully I plant trees, herbs and flowers and wet their roots with the precious drops. The cool well water attracts human beings and animals to refresh and quicken themselves. Trees give shade, the land turns green, fragrant flowers bloom, insects, birds and butterflies show their devotion to God, the creator, as if they were citing the first Sura of the Qu'ran. The human, perceiving the hidden praise of God, care for and see all that is created as a reflection of paradise on earth. For me this idea of an oasis in the middle of a hostile environment is like an image of the resurrection at dawn, after a long journey through the nightly desert. I saw it in front of me like a model before the actual work in the desert started. And yet in reality I desired even more: I wanted the whole world to develop.

We can see then that, in his childhood, Ibrahim was well grounded in his Muslim faith, in general, and in the relevant sura from the Qur'an, specifically, culminating in a vision of resurrection (societal renewal) at dawn. Ramadan, in fact, was the time when his mother told Ibrahim all the stories about the Prophet. He listened reverently and in admiration to accounts of the Prophet's suffering and endurance, to how intelligently he answered questions, and to how much confidence Prophet Muhammad had in people's ability for freedom. The image of an admirable man was created in Ibrahim's soul: very gentle and wise, very strong and resolute. Such a genealogical outlook, drawing on the wisdom of his people, pervaded his everyday approach to his university studies.

The one, the light and the judge

As it happened, while studying in Austria, and reaching out to another culture, Ibrahim fell in love with his Austrian wife-to-be, Gudrun. Their two children-to-be would be a mix of Catholic and Muslim in their background, if not their faith. When Ibrahim got to the university in Graz he joined the foreign visitors' club. During the early years, though, he felt quite lonely. So while he put a lot of energy into his studies of technical chemistry, the Qur'an accompanied him through his daily meditations, the same ones he had undertaken throughout his childhood. While Islam is a monotheic religion, Allah has a multitude of 99 different names that a Muslim like Ibrahim (2005) can meditate upon.

For one, "Allah is the patient one", so I practised patience. Because of this, these were years of inner exercise, which had led me to believe, throughout my life, that I am a "practising person". Through such inner exercises I tried to establish a relationship with Allah. I do not want to be known as a religious person, but as a striving, practising one. I had a goal, an ideal, Allah's ninety nine qualities. When a situation becomes unbelievably difficult for me I could see how small I was in relation to those names, which made things bearable. In fact, the names are divided into three sets of thirty-three, in terms of: the One (for example creator, wise, evolver, initiator), the Light (for instance watching, destroyer, expander, compassionate), and the Judge (for example strong, just, loving, forgiveness). To BE, meanwhile, is the highest ideal.

During his studies, moreover, Ibrahim noticed inner changes taking place within himself. He became thoroughly involved with European culture, getting to know its music, studying its poetry and philosophy. Somebody looking into his soul would have seen anything "Egyptian" left completely behind, so he could absorb everything new. Because of his childhood and adolescent grounding, though, in Egyptian culture, and in Islam, he could not leave this entirely behind. He now existed in two worlds, both of which were essentially different: the oriental, spiritual stream he was born into, and the European, which he felt was his chosen course. But he was neither Egyptian nor European. After he had successfully completed his PhD studies, in both pharmacy and engineering, at the University of Graz in Austria, and proceeded on to a career as a research scientist, his life took a new turn. The knowledge and spiritual base for this, as we shall see below, was anthroposophy, and the work of Rudolph Steiner, to which he had been introduced by an Austrian friend, Martha Werth.

"Wouldn't you like to come with me on a journey to Egypt?", Martha asked Ibrahim one day. She wanted to know if he had come across ancient Egyptian cultures. So he decided to take the opportunity, and to go with her. They started out in 1974, and visited Aswan, Luxor, Karnak and the Valley of the Kings. She gave him a new enthusiasm for ancient Egyptian art and mythology. Ibrahim was in fact shocked by the contrast between the greatness, wisdom and elevation shown thousands of years ago by the pharaohs, and modern Egypt. In the evenings he discussed his experiences and thoughts with Martha. She listened and asked him what he wanted to do: "What is your destiny?" For the time being he was unsure as to which way to go.

The prospect of advent of biodynamic agriculture for Egypt

A healing force: oikos and cosmos

On the return journey, in fact, Ibrahim thanked Allah that he did not live in Egypt, but in beautiful Austria with his wife and children, a son and a daughter, and his successful career, as now head of research for an Austrian pharmaceutical company. And yet he could not forget the images and encounters he had experienced. Every morning he awoke and realized anew how the events of the journey had renewed and transformed him. At the same time he continued to work with global anthroposophy, now as well as local Islam, and with in the former case spiritual, as well as material, science, also becoming acquainted with its practical applications in many walks of life, including in agriculture, education and social as well as economic enterprise.

The deeper he was able to penetrate into the matter, the more answers he received for his persistent questioning and inner restlessness. He repeatedly found life-changing solutions suddenly presenting themselves to him after intense contemplation. *Biodynamic agriculture, which is a form of organic agriculture (oikos) that works with cosmic forces (cosmos) and is based on anthroposophy, particularly fascinated him.* One day Martha Werth told him about a lecture, being given locally, by a disciple of Steiner's, George Merckens, an advisor to biodynamic farms in Austria and Italy. At last he found a friend who understood that biodynamic farming could transform Egypt's agriculture.

Liberate Egypt from its misery

Ibrahim then told his children the story of a man who decided to move to the desert with his children and who created a big garden there. Once he had painted the picture in great detail, he suddenly asked: "And what would happen if we were that family?" Spontaneously there were shouts of joy. His son was 16 and his daughter 14. His son would ride a motorbike across the desert and his daughter would ride horses. To Martha Werth he wrote a farewell letter (2005):

> *For my soul Austria was like a spiritual childhood garden. Now I hope the souls of Egyptian people can be revitalised and renewed by a garden in the desert. After establishing a farm as a healthy physical basis for soul and spiritual development, I will set up further things, following the example of human development: a kindergarten, high school, vocational education, hospital and cultural institutions. My goal is the development of humans in a comprehensive sense. I want to pass on this richness of nature and spirit to Egypt, to sow the seeds I have been given.*

In another letter (2005) he wrote to a scientist friend, Dr Zwieauer in Vienna:

> *My soul has begun to separate into two parts: an ambitious, successful part and a seeking questioning one, willing to see things in a new light, and to transform and elevate them to a new and higher level. I am consciously leaving the successful part behind me and am giving myself up to the questioning one. With this I am uniting my soul with its spiritual home and am liberating the rigidity of ambitiousness so that I am open for new tasks, encounters and goals.*

Taking people on a collective Sekem journey

Ibrahim knew that bringing down the idea of Sekem into the real world couldn't be done without the help of other people that commit deeply to the same vision. He has therefore never stopped asking Allah to send people that can contribute to the different initiatives, and knowledge creating activities. In the very early years of Sekem, Dr Hans Werner, working in the field of anthroposophic medicine, with his wife Elfriede, followed their inner voice during a visit to Egypt and, with due synchronicity, managed to find the remote location of Sekem farm where Ibrahim welcomed them with open arms. They did not know each other, but Ibrahim said, "I knew you were coming", which marked the beginning of a very deep and long-lasting friendship. Thereafter many more kindred spirits, especially from the German-speaking world, were to follow Ibrahim to Sekem.

Table 2.1 Sekem: nature, culture, society, economy

Innovation driven institutionalized research: path of renewal Sekem Commonwealth Nature, culture, society, economy

- *Communal attributes*: <u>Grounding</u> – Constituting Africa, **Sekem Commonwealth**, European Trinity; <u>Emergence</u> – social research paradigm, social ecology, integral development; <u>Navigation</u> – communitalism, integral university, reinventing knowledge; <u>Effect</u> – social economy, knowledge creation, solidarity economy.
- *Integrator role*: institutionalized research, e.g. **Ibrahim Abouleish**.
- *Research function*: scholarship, research and knowledge creation lodged in SEKEM **Social Innovation Centre**.
- <u>*Navigating knowledge creation*</u>: grounding and origination in the renewal and **reinterpretation of Islam**; emergent foundation *lodged in **the fusion between the occident (anthroposophy) and the orient (Islam)***; emancipatory **navigation through anthroposophical approach** to natural, cultural, political and economic systems; effecting the **reclamation of the desert**; thereby ultimately pursuing **sustainable development**.

Subsequent to their first visit Hans and Elfriede have come to Egypt almost every year and together they built up the Sekem medical centre and later the first European association of Sekem Friends in Germany. This network of friends and supporters played an important role in the life of Sekem and was replicated in many other European countries. This story and human encounter show *a basic characteristic of Sekem's development: it is based on people's inner motivation and commitment to contribute to something bigger than themselves, something that is to build for the future.* The art behind this is to sustain the impulse of others and keep the structures that were created and let other people grow into these new forms. The challenge is to translate this way of engaging people into the every-day operations as the abovementioned examples illustrate, albeit that they are a rather special case involving people that have found their inner call and want to realize it together with Sekem.

Sekem philosophies, structures and processes

The Sustainability Flower

As seen in Figure 2.1, Sekem's *Sustainability Flower*, which has been developed for performance monitoring and reporting purposes (Sekem Holding, 2013), is divided up between cultural, societal and economic life, altogether underpinned by nature and ecology.

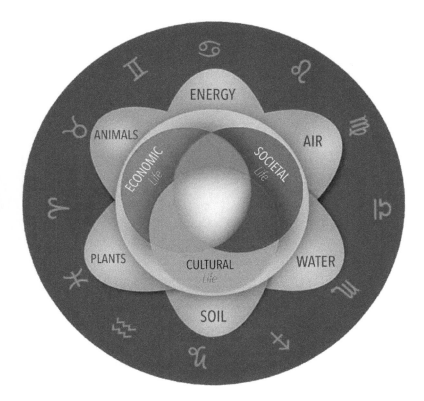

Figure 2.2 Sekem's sustainability flower.

Sekem's model for sustainable development, as it stands today, some forty years from when it was initially conceived, integrates different spheres of life, natural and social scientific disciplines, into a holistic whole where all parts are independent and interconnected.

The first three of these – cultural, societal and economic life – are drawn from Martin Large's *Commonwealth* (see opening quote above) and constitute the social organism next to the natural one (see Figure 2.3).

Sekem's fourfold commonwealth

As Sekem's natural and social, functional and structural vision stands today:

- *we establish biodynamic agriculture as the competitive solution for the environmental, social and food security challenges of the 21st century;*

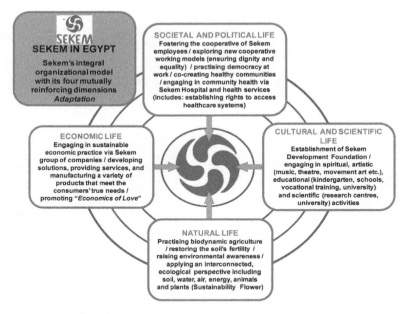

Figure 2.3 Sekem as an integral enterprise.

- *we build successful business models in accordance with ecological and ethical principles;*
- *we want to provide products and services of the highest standards to meet the needs of the consumer.*

The intertwined natural, social, cultural and economic realms of activity within Sekem's group of companies begins on a practical level by healing the soil through the application of biodynamic farming methods. Biodynamic agriculture stands for a self-containing and self-sustaining eco-system without any unnatural additions. Soil, plants, animals and humans together create an image of a holistic living organism. Sekem's approach of sustainable agriculture includes the regenerative powers of agriculture. The very fact that Sekem's approach turns desert into living soils through the application of compost and biodynamic methods, shows that desert land can be reclaimed and thus regenerated. For more than thirty-five years, Sekem has been building up living soils in desert land and implementing closed nutrient cycles with livestock integration and a diverse range of crops, plants and trees. By farming without chemicals, the health of the farmers and the consumers who eat organic products regenerates. The returning wildlife also benefits, which in turn gives back to the farm by helping to keep down insect pests.

Sekem's approach to agriculture stands in direct contrast to business-as-usual industrial agriculture. The latter relies heavily on external inputs, spreads vast areas of monocultures over the planet, and even changes the plants' genetic source codes to increase resistance to pests and adaptation to climate change. Numerous scientific studies have shown, however, that industrial agriculture and the application of genetically modified organisms (GMOs) affects the ecosystems negatively and in fact rather degrades than regenerates them.

Sekem's socio-political vision here states:

- *we create workplaces reflecting human dignity and supporting employee development;*
- *we locally and globally advocate for a holistic approach to sustainable development;*
- *we build a long-term, trusting and fair relationship with our partners.*

Sekem as it is today

Sekem aims to establish a blueprint for the healthy corporation of the twenty-first century, albeit one that, as of 2012, also included a university for sustainable development. To begin with, as such, it was the first entity to apply biodynamic farming methods in Egypt. Its commitment to innovative development thereby led to the nationwide application of biodynamic methods to control pests and improve crop yields. In that guise it functioned as a veritable agricultural and ecological laboratory. Sekem has since grown exponentially into a nationally renowned enterprise and market leader of organic products and phyto-pharmaceuticals, which are now also exported to Europe and other countries.

The Sekem group that represents the economic branch of the initiative, includes a holding company with five main subsidiaries: Sekem for Land Reclamation for farming and organic seedlings, fertilization and pest control; Isis for fresh fruits and vegetables as well as for organic foods and beverages (such as juice, dairy products, oils, spices and tea); Lotus for medical plants, herbs and spices; NatureTex for organic cotton and textile children's clothes and home wear; and Atos for phyto-pharmaceutical products; and now also the university.

Sekem, then, has a highly unconventional business model that incorporates what are usually considered social and environmental externalities and in fact maintains this to be the basis for an increasing competitiveness in the future. While it is a profit-making enterprise, it does not aim for profit maximization. Through a fair trade approach, it shares the value created with the smallholder farmers in its network called the Egyptian Biodynamic Association (EBDA). Furthermore, 10 per cent of Sekem's profit goes to the Sekem Development Foundation (SDF) that has launched many beneficial community development initiatives. These include its primary, secondary and vocational schools as well as its university for sustainable development, and its medical centre, altogether celebrating culture and diversity, and promoting peace, cooperation and understanding between all human beings.

Conclusion: Sekem addressing societal challenges

Sustainable desert reclamation

The societal challenges of Egypt – such as climate change, resource scarcity, population growth, extreme poverty, absence of food security – need innovative, problem-solving solutions. In that context it is important to realize that the Energy–Water–Food nexus represents a huge challenge for sustainable development in Egypt and agriculture is strongly related to that. Sustainable desert reclamation plays a key role in addressing those challenges and therefore contributing to political stability and the related transition towards an authentic form of democracy. This is relevant not only for Egypt but for the whole region.

Stewardship of the Earth

It is within this context of food insecurity and social and environmental challenges that Sekem represents a viable economic – if not also "polity" – alternative, one that builds upon a praxis of sustainable agriculture that resonates strongly with Muslim insights and teachings, for example those related to stewardship (Lessem *et al.*, 2015). Stewardship (*Khalifa*), moreover, implies social equality and dignity of all human beings – regardless of skin colour, social status, etc. – a cardinal element of the Islamic faith. Within this, the right attitude towards others is not "might is right", the struggle to serve one's own self-interest, or "the struggle to survive", but rather mutual cooperation, to develop the entire human potential. Second, resources are a trust (*amanah*), provided by Allah, whereby the human being is not the primary owner, but is just a trustee (*amin*). So resources are for the benefit of all, for the wellbeing not just for oneself and one's family, but for the community at large. This includes the whole web of life, from soil organisms to insects, birds, wildlife and plant life, as explained in the Qur'an:

006:038 There is not an animal (that lives) on the earth, nor a being that flies on its wings, but (forms part of) communities like you. Nothing have We omitted from the Book, and they (all) shall be gathered to their Lord in the end.

Research structure and functioning

In the final analysis, though, Sekem, while being a veritable development sanctuary, at its founding core, lodged in many an Egyptian desert community, while functioning as an ongoing natural, cultural, socio-technical laboratory, also recently establishing a university, has not yet configured itself as an integrated inter-institutional genealogy as such. This in fact has been the intention of its so-called Social Innovation Centre, to spearhead such an integral development.

We now turn from Sekem as a commonwealth, on the path of renewal, to what we term the European Trinity, on the path of reasoned realization, all with a view to Grounding innovation driven, institutionalized research. In Chapter 8, moreover, we shall focus on Heliopolis University for Sustainable Development, as an offshoot of Sekem, and would-be Integral University, as also a stepping stone, if you like, towards an Institutional Genealogy (Chapter 9).

References

Abouleish, I. (2005) *Sekem: A Sustainable Community in the Egyptian Desert.* Edinburgh: Floris Publications.

Karenga, M. (2005) *Maat: The Moral Ideal in Ancient Egypt.* London: Routledge.

Large, M. (2013) *Commonwealth: For a Free, Equal, Mutual and Sustainable Society.* Stroud: Hawthorne Press.

Lessem, R., Abouleish, I., Pogacnik, M. and Herman, L. (2015) *Integral Polity: Aligning Nature, Culture, Society and Economy.* Abingdon. Routledge

Sekem Holding (2013) *Sekem Report on Sustainable Development 2012,* August 2013. At www.sekem.com/rsd (accessed December 2016).

3 European Trinity

A classical perspective on creative innovation

Summary of chapter:

1   institutionalized research is grounded in truth, goodness and beauty;
2   it emerges through scientific, managerial and artistic creativity;
3   it is navigated via phases of creativity, elaboration and orientation;
4   it is effected by nine innovators – entrepreneurial innovator to artistic certifier,
5   Europe emerges out of the innovation shadows into the light.

Introduction: path of reasoned realization of institutional research

"Southern" relational to "north-western" realization

We now turn from relational grounding in Africa, in the South, then onto the path of renewal in the Middle East, now onto prospectively reasoned realization in Europe. While then in *Constituting* Africa we revisited, *relationally* and descriptively via Chancellor Williams, its constitutional, judicial, legal and educational origins, through the Sekem *Commonwealth* we discovered, narratively via Sekem and Abouleish, how the ancient cross-roads of civilizations, Egypt, could be ecologically and economically, socially and politically, *renewed*. In both cases, moreover, this was with an eye to (but not yet realized) the *grounding* of *innovation driven, institutionalized research*, functionally, and structurally within an *inter-institutionalized genealogy*.

We now look to classically European "north-western" innovation-driven research, so to speak, albeit based now on the ancient Greek trinity of truth, beauty and goodness. This now culminates trans-disciplinary grounding of the *reasoned-realization* path in science, and in art, or and ethics, or management.

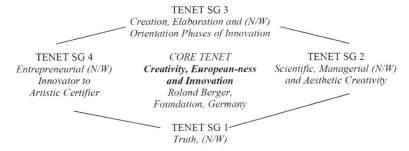

TENET SG 3
Creation, Elaboration and (N/W)
Orientation Phases of Innovation

TENET SG 4	CORE TENET	TENET SG 2
Entrepreneurial (N/W)	**Creativity, European-ness**	*Scientific, Managerial (N/W)*
Innovator to	**and Innovation**	*and Aesthetic Creativity*
Artistic Certifier	*Roland Berger,*	
	Foundation, Germany	

TENET SG 1
Truth, (N/W)

Figure 3.1 Institutional reasoned research: grounding tenets.

European Trinity and four quadrants

In fact for renowned American contemporary social philosopher Ken Wilber, whose *Integral Theory* (2006) we focused on in the previous volume, *Awakening Integral Consciousness*, all major languages have what are called first-, second- and third-person pronouns. The first-person perspective refers to "the person who is speaking", that is, *I* (singular) and *we* (plural). The second, the "person who is spoken to", includes pronouns like *you*. The third, the "person that is spoken about", is *him* or *her* or *they* and *them*, if not *it*. As specifically then the <u>third</u> person, or "it" in fact, represents objective <u>Truth</u>, it is best investigated by science (Wilber, as we shall see below, then distinguishes between "it" single and "its" plural). The <u>second</u> person or you/we refers to <u>Goodness</u> or the way we treat each other, in other words with basic morality. And the <u>first</u> person deals with I, with self-expression, art, <u>Beauty</u> and aesthetics. So the "I", "we" and "it" dimension refer to art, morals and science respectively; self, culture and nature; or beauty, goodness and truth.

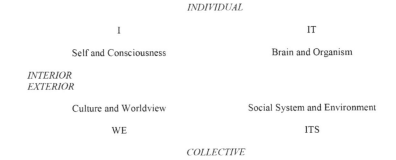

INDIVIDUAL

I	IT
Self and Consciousness	Brain and Organism

INTERIOR
EXTERIOR

Culture and Worldview	Social System and Environment
WE	ITS

COLLECTIVE

Figure 3.2 Wilber's four quadrants.

This altogether constitutes Wilber's four quadrants, or four different worldviews, which can be likened to our integral *realms*; for him the inside and outside of the individual and the collective; the "I", the "we", and two "its" – singular and plural.

Light and shadow: breakthrough innovation shaping European business

Meanwhile in the 1990s, in Europe in fact, a group of management researchers, from the UK (myself), Germany (including a coordinating consultant from Roland Berger itself), France, Italy and Spain, as well as from the US (Philip Rosenzweig from Harvard and now based at IMD) and Japan (the renowned author – see Chapter 11 – of the knowledge creating company, Ikujiro Nonaka), gathered together. Sponsored by Germany's Roland Berger Foundation (Roland Berger is one of Europe's largest strategic consultancies) in Munich, we focused topically then on European-ness and Innovation.

Three years of our subsequent group (though not institutionalized) research was then featured in our book that came out in the mid-1990s: *The Light and the Shadow: Breakthrough Innovation Shaping European Business* (1996). Needless to say, we lacked an institutional genealogy to go with it, and thereby lacked sustainability (see Conclusion below).

In the opening chapter of our book, we management researchers wrote:

> *as we enter the knowledge era we, in business in Europe, ignore our heritage to our peril. For unless we reach into our own roots* (in the shadow), *and evolve from them, we will forever be bound to others, most notably the Americans and the Japanese* (in the light).

Today in fact China may have eclipsed Japan, but, that aside, those words ring all too true some two decades later, and we shall see at the end of this chapter the responsibility we bore for this. Moreover, and interestingly enough, Chancellor Williams (see Chapter 1) was saying the same about Africa, in the 1970s, as we were saying about Europe, in the 1990s: that Africa and Europe, if not also the Middle East, needed to draw more purposefully, institutionally, on its genealogy.

From Socrates and Abelard to Adam Smith

The European quest for knowledge, if not also its institutionalization, began in ancient Athens in the age of Socrates, albeit that many, like Maulana Karenga (see Chapter 2) would argue that ancient Athens in Europe drew in turn on ancient Egypt in Africa. It was Socrates, arguably then, who first steered the course of human oral inquiry (see also Chapter 9 on Institutional Genealogy) towards things of the physical world rather than the gods and supernatural phenomena; it was the student of Socrates, Plato, who first elaborated in writing a set of ideals that humanity could reach through art, science and design. In effect, *truth, goodness and beauty were the three ideals that Plato viewed as being the goals of a just society*. The pursuit of these fundamentals has occupied European innovators in every sphere of thought, feeling and action ever since.

By the year AD 1107 Paris – today in the autumn of 2016 lying at the European heart of "global terrorism" – had become famous as the European centre of learning. Whereas conventional wisdom at the time agreed with St Anselm, "I believe therefore I know", a young scholar and theologian Peter Abelard (embarking on a passionate love affair with one of his female pupils, the poor man was castrated by a vengeful uncle) challenged this wisdom. *By doubting we come to examine, and by examining so we perceive the truth*. Repeatedly condemned by the Catholic Church, Abelard nevertheless set the spirit of inquiry that led to the discoveries of Descartes and Newton five centuries later. Today we call this *the path of reasoned realization* in pursuit of innovation driven, institutionalized research, functionally, by way of "north-western" grounding on truth, goodness and beauty, navigated through an institutional genealogy (Lessem and Schieffer, 2010).

In 1434 Prince Henry the Navigator of Portugal set out to explore the limits of the known world, marking a period of European discovery, not to mention also his participation in colonialism. From being an expanse of unknown, the world quickly became a vast frontier where men ventured forth, and indeed exploited physical and human resources. World trade, in the sixteenth and seventeenth centuries, became the new frontier of discovery and imagination, while also heralding such an age of colonial exploitation, including the advent of African slavery. Indeed every path has its downside if isolated from the others, in this case reasoned realization set apart from the relational path and that of renewal. As economies grew they became more complex, and this led in turn to further increases in wealth. That paved the way in 1776 for a 53-year-old Scottish academic, Adam Smith, to say (often contested) that *the invisible hand of the market, without intending it, without knowing it, advances the interests of society*. Indeed we call such "self-interested" thereby "western" approach to scientific research as well as to economic development, the path of *realization* (Lessem and Schieffer, 2010).

Smith was not so much an innovator as a catalyst for thought and development, who synthesized a previously disorganized field and made it into a discipline. From Smith came the three factors of production – land, labour and capital. His influence was further strengthened by relating his economic ideas to the moral dimension of human action, the latter by and large having got lost along the way.

The advent of institutionalization

Among the greatest of European innovations, though, is that of the "north-western" corporation, and thereby the institutionalization of enterprise, at least in this case in a business context. The prototypes of such were established in northern Italy around the time of the first notorious crusade (1096), having their origin in high-value, high-risk trade in eastern goods between Europe and Asia. Indeed, at the same time, the first European universities were being established there. Companies were therefore founded as societies of traders banding together to invest capital, take advantage of economies of scale and share risk.

By the fourteenth century every major European centre had its stock exchange and double-entry accounting had been established by the Renaissance scholar Luca Pacioli, together with the forerunners of modern business schools – teaching standard business practices. Banking had become increasingly sophisticated with the introduction of notes of exchange and European-wide systems of credit.

Business meanwhile had become truly international, one Genoese firm having agents working, for example, in Iceland and China. The challenge then presented by the European "north-west" to the "rest" was how to develop complementary institutions of their "eastern" and "southern" own. Arguably, to this day, whereas the Japanese "east" at the turn of the last century rose to that occasion, the "global south" has not succeeded, by and large, in developing its own indigenous, if not also exogenous, large-scale organizations, as per our structurally based *institutional genealogy*, which of course affects our overall prospect of innovation driven, *institutionalized*, research.

We now turn to knowledge and functionally based research-and-innovation.

Knowledge and innovation in Europe

Truth, goodness and beauty

Plato was the first European, as we have seen, to reconcile all the various aspects of knowledge, in an early European version of our integral realms. *Truth, goodness and beauty, for Europeans as such, are what freedom is for the Americans, or harmony for the Asians, or ntu (vital force) for Africans.* In Figure 3.3 below we articulate such a *European Trinity*.

Truth

Reason
Logic
Technological Progress

Knowledge

Goodness

Moral Judgement
Efficiency/utility
Management

Beauty

Intuition
Aesthetic Appeal
Design

Figure 3.3 The European Trinity.

In what follows, then, we relate such a European Trinity of "knowledge sources" to a standard lifecycle of innovation, in fact the one proposed by the Roland Berger strategic consultants who formed part of our research group.

Sources of knowledge

Knowledge, for the strategic consultants, can be newly created, or existing knowledge can simply be made more widely available. Such knowledge, in either case, becomes valuable when ideas can be related. While this is then the key ingredient of innovation, place and time are also critical ingredients, which is where, as we shall see below, our "Cultural Compass" (Lessem and Neubauer, 1993) comes in, further evolved through the *Integral Worldviews* – realities, realms, rhythm and rounds – that Trans4m has subsequently developed. Different cultures, in their respective places then, have different concepts of knowledge and learning. Time herein refers to the innovation lifecycle, that is, *creation, elaboration and orientation.*

European-ness and innovation

Invention and innovation: individual and collective

Innovation, for our primarily European, but also American and Japanese management researchers then, involved the generation and application of new knowledge. To many, innovation is synonymous with technological advancement, but there are innumerable varieties of innovation. Ideas are often inter-disciplinary or cross-functional in nature. Creative people tend to be cosmopolitan and boundary crossing. Unlike invention, which is often an individual effort, innovation – inclusive of commercialization – results from collective effort.

Types of innovation: technological, managerial, aesthetic

All innovations, following Plato in a European context as we saw above, can be roughly divided into three types: those seeking excellence through alternately *aesthetic appeal* (beauty), *managerial innovations* (goodness), or – most commonly recognized – scientific discovery or *technological advancement* (truth). It is interesting then to note that for our group of researchers, management was identified with "goodness" (arguably aligned with Europe's "social" orientation), and thereby inherently had an underlying moral basis to it.

Innovation and time: creation, elaboration, orientation

In the first *creation* stage, for Roland Berger as management consultants then, often associated with business start-ups, firms are concerned with the immediate exploitation of good ideas. Frequently this idea has been the genesis of the firm itself. The second stage, *elaboration*, is more complex. Now the enterprise needs to defend itself against the competition while simultaneously developing a new tranche of innovations.

Table 3.1 Creativity, European-ness and innovation

Innovation driven institutionalized research: reasoned realization
Reframes knowledge through innovative social science and humanities
Contributes to breakthrough European innovation

- *Communal attributes*: <u>Grounding</u> – Constituting Africa, Sekem Commonwealth, **European Trinity**; <u>Emergence</u> – social research paradigm, social ecology, integral development; <u>Navigation</u> – communitalism, integral university, reinventing knowledge; <u>Effect</u> – social economy, knowledge creation, solidarity economy.
- *Integrator role*: researcher/innovator, e.g. **Roland Berger Foundation**.
- *Research function*: scholarship, research on **European-ness/Innovation**.
- *Navigating knowledge creation*: Such innovation driven institutionalized research is grounded in **truth, goodness and beauty**; emerges through **scientific, managerial and artistic creativity**; is navigated through innovation phases of **creativity, elaboration and orientation**; is effected through nine types of innovator ranging from **entrepreneurial innovator to artistic certifier**, culminating in **Europe emerging out of the innovation shadows into the light.**

By this stage it is assumed that the firm has copied and even improved on the original innovation. Finally, *orientation* is the stage where the firm contemplates the future and plans how it will use its innovative capabilities to meet challenges and create opportunities. This is the visionary stage, which needs a special kind of leadership (see Figure 3.6 below). We now proceed to combine the European Trinity, as above, the process of innovation, and our own integral worlds – specifically our integral *realities* – that we outlined in our previous volume on *Awakening Integral Consciousness* (1996).

Diversity as a source of innovation

Cultural and corporate compass

Universal determinants of innovation are not in doubt. What is particular to our work, though, set in a European context, is the importance of cultural diversity, on the one hand, as well as an overall European genealogy, on the other. As such we turn to our *cultural compass*, embodied in our "integral realities/worldviews" (see *Awakening Integral Consciousness*, Chapter 4). In this way *rational* northern cultures emphasize technological vision and industrial enterprise. This is the case, for example, in technology-based company Trumpf, one of the world's biggest providers of machine tools, in Germany. *Humanistic* southern cultures have a founding vision that is based on the organization, as is the case for the world's most renowned group of cooperatives *Mondragon* (see Chapter 10) in the Basque country in Spain. There is a strong emphasis on cooperation, constitutionally and managerially, and on an overall communitarian approach.

Eastern *holistic* cultures identify with society as a whole, and with a network of organizations as an interdependent organism, as is characteristic of Japan's *Kao*, engaged in beauty care, home care and surface chemicals as a whole in Japan. Finally, *pragmatic* Western companies, such as the software giant Microsoft in the US, focus their innovativeness on creative responses to the market. The cultural compass, moreover, can be related to both spheres and phases of innovation, as is illustrated below.

Subjective and objective spheres of innovation

Knowledge-contingent innovation then reflects personal and organizational visions and interpretations of the ideals of truth, goodness and beauty, also incorporating "northern" objectivity and "southern" subjectivity (see Figure 3.4):

Figure 3.4 Northern objectivity and southern subjectivity.

Cultural styles and corporate evolution

Time-contingent innovation reflects the current stage in the corporate lifecycle corresponding with the needs for creation, elaboration and orientation. The initial stages of business foundation and survival tend to be more action oriented (western), whereas later stages call for a relatively greater emphasis on communication and vision (eastern).

We are now ready to conclude, ultimately alas on a melancholy note.

Conclusion: European innovation found and lost

European Innovation Typology

The overall European *Innovation Typology* that our research group came up with, then (Roland Berger Foundation, 1996), forged out of the knowledge sources (truth, goodness, beauty) and innovation process (creation, elaboration, orientation), duly aligned with our integral realities, was the one below.

Overall then, and in the light ultimately of this, thereby grounding *reasoned-realization* institutionalized research, *such research is originated in truth, goodness and beauty; is founded upon scientific, managerial and artistic creativity; is navigated via phases of creativity, elaboration and orientation; is transformatively effected by nine types of innovators – from entrepreneurial innovator to artistic certifier – whereby Europe emerges out of the innovation shadows into the light.*

Figure 3.5 Western action and eastern vision.

	CREATION	ELABORATION	ORIENTATION
TECHNOLOGICAL PROGRESS	Entrepreneurial Inventor	Managerial Engineer	Technological Visionary
MANAGERIAL INNOVATION	Opportunistic Mover	Systems Architect	Socio-Economic Philosopher
AESTHETIC APPEAL	Gifted Creative	Charismatic Moderator	Artistic Certifier

Figure 3.6 European innovator typology.

Alas, at least in our Roland Berger foundational context, European innovation did not emerge out of the shadows, despite our innovation driven research. Why so?

Europe's lost genealogy in business and management circles

Take a look now at Roland Berger, Foundation and Consultancy, as of 2016. As far as the Foundation is first concerned, as we can see on their website (2016), typical indeed of a conventionally "western" corporation and consultancy today, in its annual Foundation awards for champions of Human Rights,

> *Roland Berger Foundation pays tribute to individuals and organizations from around the world who have dedicated themselves to opposing* <u>*human rights*</u> *violations in whatever form. We wish to acknowledge their untiring efforts to defend human dignity and to work for tolerance and peace in human interaction. For they are not diverted from their path by the lack of awareness of those around them, by setbacks and even, in some cases, by threats to their life*

Now if we turn to Roland Berger Consultancy itself (2016), one of Europe's largest consultancies,

> *Our corporate culture is based on three fundamental values:* <u>*entrepreneurship, excellence and empathy.*</u> *We at Roland Berger are committed to these core values. They constitute the foundation of our professional work, our interaction with our clients, business partners and communities, and define our entire corporate culture.*

We are capable of understanding <u>entrepreneurial</u> challenges, and know what makes successful entrepreneurs in all markets. This means actively exploring unconventional ideas, taking risks and blazing new trails, but also means willingness to assume responsibility. We encourage our employees to take responsibility for business decisions early on in their career. All of us are eager to find innovative and sustainable solutions to help our clients be "game-changers" in their environment.

We achieve <u>excellent results</u> and develop global best practices to ensure both measurable and sustainable success. Our goal is excellence in our work with clients, in the way we develop our knowledge and in our interaction with each other – externally and internally. To do so, we challenge ourselves time and again. We appreciate brilliant minds that create sound analyses and fact-based approaches. Investing in our employees' development is essential to ensure outstanding results for our clients and build long-lasting relationships with them. We value open discussion and debate in decision-making until the best outcome has been achieved.

We place ourselves in your position to be able to act as <u>insightful, respectful and responsible</u> advisors. Roland Berger employees offer a unique combination of intellectual and emotional competence to really meet our clients' aims and needs. We act as partners alongside our clients and focus on understanding the real problem, offering peer-to-peer advice and tailored approaches. Our firm is committed to tolerance and respect. We value diversity as a strength within our own company and know how to thrive on diversity in our clients' environment. Appreciating others' perspectives and feedback, we take all stakeholders into careful consideration and respond with integrity to the trust our clients place in us.

Well, those "Three E's" – Entrepreneurship, Excellence and Empathy – could be qualities of any strategic consultancy anywhere in the world. In other words, in the new millennium, they have completely lost touch with the European Trinity – Truth, Goodness and Beauty – that we had revisited and reviewed with them in the 1990s. No wonder Europe, economically, continues to lie in the shadows of the United States and now also China! In such socio-economic guise it has seemingly completely lost touch with its cultural heritage, whereby, with truth (science) and beauty (art) each ploughing their separate furrows, unifying goodness (management) is nowhere to be seen.

The problem of course is, for Europe, that the book we produced on the matter (Roland Berger Foundation, 1996) has been subsequently totally ignored by Roland Berger specifically and by the European management establishment – both academics and practitioners – generally. In fact we only found a publisher for it because the owner of the publishing company, Capstone in Oxford at the time (1996) in fact, happened to be a personal colleague and friend who had published many of my previous books when he was a commissioning editor at Blackwells in Oxford. More specifically, it was not the book per se that was by-passed but the *institutional genealogy* that would need to have been co-evolved among Roland Berger Foundation as *sanctuary* so to speak, Roland Berger Consultancy as *laboratory*, a management research group as representative of a *research university*, and one or other constituent European *community*. No such genealogy transpired.

This, then, tells its own story of why Europe continues to be in the economic shadows, and, in terms of innovation driven, institutionalized research, the same applies to Africa and the Middle East! And that is precisely why we need to purposefully build up innovation driven, institutionalized social research, genealogically and ultimately institutionally from the ground up. We therefore now turn from the initial grounding of innovation driven institutionalized social research, *relationally* (southern), *renewal wise* (eastern) and *through reasoned realization* (north-western), to further emergence of such, initially, and thereby relationally, through a would-be Communitalism/Communiversity in Nigeria.

References

Lessem, R. and Neubauer, F. (1993) *European Management Systems*. Maidenhead: McGraw Hill.

Lessem, R. and Schieffer, A. (2010) *Integral Research and Innovation*. Abingdon: Routledge.

Roland Berger Consultancy (2016) Values. At https://www.rolandberger.com/en/about/Values.html (accessed December 2016).

Roland Berger Foundation (1996) *The Light and the Shadow: Breakthrough Innovation Shaping European Business*. Oxford: Capstone.

Roland Berger Foundation (2016) Philosophy. At http://www.rolandbergerstiftung.org/en/the-foundation/philosophy/ (accessed December 2016).

Wilber, K. (2006) *Integral Spirituality*. Boston, MA: Integral Books.

Part II

Emergence of institutionalized research

4 Communitalism

A communal and relational perspective on Pax Africana

Summary of chapter:

1   Pax Natura embedded in nature and community – southern humanism;
2   Pax Spiritus as sanctuary embodying culture and spirituality – eastern holism;
3   Pax Scientia as university – science and technology, northern rationalism;
4   Pax Economia as laboratory – economy and enterprise, western pragmatism;
5   each form of genealogy ultimately complementing the other.

Introduction: social research and innovation

In the previous three chapters, on grounding institutionalized research, relationally in the African "south", renewal wise in the middle "east", and reasoned realization wise in the European "north-west", we laid the innovation driven research grounds, locally and functionally so to speak, if not also genealogically and structurally, in each African, Middle Eastern and European case, for what is now locally–globally to emerge. Indeed we shall now pave the emergent institutional way, more purposefully as a bridge between grounding and navigation, in Nigeria, in Zimbabwe and in Slovenia for what is more fully to come, emancipatory wise, building on what has come before. We start then, relationally, with an emerging *Communitalism*, along the way to *Pax Africana*, building on what has come functionally hitherto in our opening research-based chapter, "Constituting the South".

Our approach to integral research (Lessem and Schieffer, 2010), which we shall be focusing on more specifically in Chapter 7, for Dr Anselm Adodo (Adodo, 2017), founder of Paxherbals in rural Nigeria (whom we initially met in our first volume, *Community Activation for Integral Development*), has been conceived precisely because social research rarely leads to social innovation that addresses the needs, and is based on the unique gifts, of a particular society. So pervasive is the achievement of the physical sciences, as Chancellor Williams has intimated in our opening chapter, that the words technology and innovation are often used solely in connection with the physical sciences. The idea of a social scientist being an "innovator", both in functional and structural terms, as has been the case for Father Anselm Adodo, might therefore sound strange to most people, not to mention the fact that Adodo is born and bred in Africa, rather than Europe or America.

So often, for Adodo then, social research tends to remain a mere intellectual exercise with no measureable social impact. The problem is that such research, for him, is invariably built on an incomplete empirical–rational foundation, a skewed methodology that is heavily biased towards the West and the North (America and Europe), and systematically neglects the more relational and holistic South and East (Africa and Asia). Yet, the foundation and origin of civilization lies in the south. The only way forward, Adodo argues, is for research to go back to origins, including for Williams thereby *Reconstituting Africa*, the true meaning of "religare", being to reconnect with the foundation story of humanity, in order to chart a meaningful path forward, towards the future. We now turn from Constituting Africa in general to Pax Herbals functionally as well as structurally, specifically.

Paxherbals and Pax Africana

Grounded in nature and community

Through the utilization of common plants and weeds, Pax Herbal Clinic and Research Laboratories (Paxherbals), a centre for scientific cultivation, identification and development of African Medicine founded in 1996, as we saw in our first CARE volume, was able to develop a natural science-based approach to developing herbal recipes that has been of help to the local community and to millions of Nigerians. It also has a home-grown business model (structure and functioning) that puts the interest of the local community as its focal point. Rather than practise capitalist "free enterprise", which encourages the individual to acquire as much for himself as possible, Paxherbals has developed a model based on what is termed *communitalism*.

Nature and community to communitalism

The term *communitalism* is functionally different, for Adodo, from communalism or indeed communism. *Communitalism* affirms that some aspects of capitalism, such as individual inventiveness, are worth pursuing and supporting, but such inventiveness must be put at the service of the community, so that both the individual and the community prosper. The key philosophy of *communitalism* is, "we are either happy together as a prosperous community or unhappy together" and thereby unprosperous. For *communitalism*, the health and prosperity of the individual cannot be separated from the health and prosperity of the local community. Global health must start from local health, not the other way round. In the process the link between individual, community and enterprise health and whole-making, functionally, will be made.

As a flourishing model of health and business enterprise, then, within a particular local community, in Edo State adjacent to Benin City in Nigeria, *Paxherbals* is activating the local community towards integral ecological and economic, scientific and cultural development. A flourishing agribusiness that allows all families in Ewu local community to engage in profitable cultivation of foodstuffs, medicinal plants and other cash crops will make the village into an economic hub. When there is an improvement in the material wellbeing of the community, the health of the members of the community will also improve. This is the essence of community medicine. Unlike bio-health, which tends to focus on disease and neglect the root cause of diseases, such as financial inequality, unjust wages, unfair working conditions, dysfunctional literacy etc., community medicine adopts an integral approach to health and wellbeing.

Communitalism to Pax Africana

Pax Natura to Economica

Altogether for Adodo then, integrally as such, thereby functionally embracing worldviews, or realities, from all four corners of the globe, drawing on our *Integral Dynamics: Cultural Dynamics, Political Economy and the Future of the University* (Lessem, *et al.*, 2013), he identifies:

Pax Natura: *south*, identified with *Africa*. Key features are: indigenous knowledge, community activation, agronomy, connection with the soil, respect and oneness with nature, a communiversity of life. Functional orientation is towards *Nature* and *Community*; structural orientation towards *Learning Community* as per EDMCS in Ewu Community.

Pax Spiritus: *east*, identified mainly with *Asia*. Key features are: emphasis on inner peace, wholeness, culture, inner security, spirituality, higher consciousness, intuition, feelings and emotions as part of human experience. Functional orientation is towards *Holism*; structural orientation towards *Developmental Sanctuary* as per Benedictine Monastery.

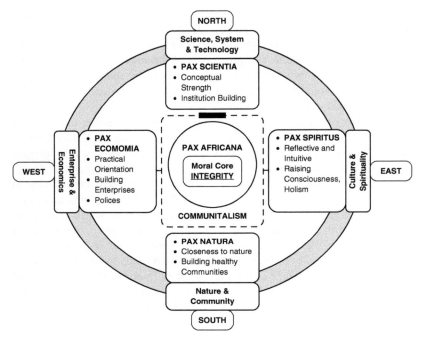

Figure 4.1 Pax natura, spiritus, scientia, economica.

Pax Scientia: *north*, identified mainly with *Europe*. Fully in control of advances in scientific theories and social theories. Key features are: political systems, educational and research outputs, and control of world's economic, political and social systems through colonization, capitalism, socialism, neo-liberalism, globalization. Functional orientation is towards *Rationalism*; structural orientation towards *Research Academy as per ACIRD* (see below).

Pax Economia: *west*, identified mainly with *America*. Known for business, enterprise, entrepreneurship, individual quest for profit and competition. Key features are: practical application of technology for profit, business management and dollarization of world economy. Functional orientation is towards *Pragmatism*; structural orientation is towards *Social and Medical Healing Laboratory as per Paxherbals*.

Communitalism and Pax

Communitalism more specifically, then, is a theory of interconnected knowledge, building further on the cooperative spirit that Chancellor

Table 4.1 Towards a communiversity/institutional genealogy

Innovation driven institutional research: emergent relational path Pax natura, Pax spiritus, Pax scientia, Pax economia Towards an institutional genealogy
• *Communal attributes*: <u>Grounding</u> – Constituting Africa, Sekem Commonwealth, European Trinity; <u>Emergence</u> – social research paradigm, social ecology, integral development, *communitalism*; <u>Navigation</u> – communitalism, integral university, reinventing knowledge; <u>Effect</u> – social economy, knowledge creation, solidarity economy. • *Integrator role*: researcher and innovator, e.g. *Dr Anselm Adodo*. • *Research function*: *Pax scientia*. • *Communitalism*: *Pax natura* embedded in nature and *community* encompassing southern humanism; *pax spiritus* as *sanctuary* embodying culture and spirituality encompassing eastern holism; *pax scientia* as *university* built upon science and technology encompassing northern rationalism; *pax economia* as *laboratory* representing economy and enterprise western pragmatism; *each form of genealogy ultimately complementing the other.*

Williams introduced us to earlier (Chapter 1). It states that knowledge is only complete and liberating when, as indicated above, it is a combination of *Pax Natura, Pax Spiritus, Pax Scientia, and Pax Economia*.

Pax is a Latin word that means *peace*. *Pax* has over the years become the *motto* of the Catholic Benedictine order of Monks. St. Benedict in his rule encouraged his monks to "listen" daily to the word of God. Listening is an art. It's something we learn to do. It is a skill. Listening requires that I lay aside my opinions and prejudices and *hear* what is being communicated to me. There are many means of communication. Speech is only one of them. In fact, only a limited proportion of human communication is done through speech. The rest is done through gestures, body movements, facial expressions and our attitudes.

When we have peace, we see things in the right way and we are able to love God and love our neighbour. The cultivation of Peace, then, is the aim of every monk. Peace does not just refer to absence of war or strife. Peace is an attitude of the soul, whereby one first accepts one's place in the world, and gives to God the honour and glory that belong to God, and gives to others the respect and honour that is due to them. Peace comes when we transcend our fears by accepting our place in the universe, and accept others as they are. Fear is a source of violence and war. When we have peace, we stop harming others. We begin to relate to others and people with honour and dignity. We stop exploiting and cheating others. This is what *Pax* is all about: communitalism in action. How, then, does this work?

Pax Africana

Communitalism in action

For Adodo, then, at *Paxherbals*, they cultivate their own herbs directly and also through accredited local outgrowers. They know the herbs, where they live, where they grow and how they grow. They know their names, their family and their story. They journey with the herbs from the farm, to the collection and verification rooms, to the washing room, drying room, the processing factory, to the final product, and to the market. They continue the journey by monitoring how the finished products interact with society, the reactions as well as the counter-reactions. To this effect, they have pharmaco-vigilance centres located in three major Nigeria cities. They ensure that we maintain this connection with the soil, with nature, the community, the environment, with the people and with science. The inability to maintain this connection is the main reason behind the crisis rocking the modern world.

Paxherbals is the only herbal manufacturing company left in Nigeria that is locally producing its herbal medicines, despite the harsh economic climate that makes it easier and more profitable to be an importer rather than a manufacturer. It is no wonder that the Nigerian market is flooded with herbal products imported from foreign countries. By so doing, Nigeria is creating wealth abroad and promoting poverty at home. *Paxherbals* believe that the only way to sustainable development is for Africa to produce what it consumes and consume what it produces. But to produce, one must innovate. *Paxherbals* is determined to continue to champion the preservation of Africa indigenous knowledge, for the sake of posterity, of African medicine, and for the sake of PAX AFRICANA, its Africa *Centre for Integral Research and Development (ACIRD)*.

ACIRD: Paxherbals to Pax Africana

The goal of ACIRD is to establish new templates for doing research *in* and *for* Africa. For centuries, according to Adodo, Africans were a people spoken about, spoken for and spoken against by foreigners. We read about who we are from what others said and wrote about us. ACIRD seeks to assert the right of Africans to speak in their own language and metaphors. We must reclaim our right to cognitive freedom, if we truly seek to be free. Africa must be aware of, and fight against, the *coloniality of knowledge* and *Epistemicide*, which are modern forms of colonization, by evolving and *e-ducing* (origin of the word education) its own research methods and research methodologies, indeed its own innovation driven institutionalized research, *suited to* and *geared towards* African epistemological emancipation.

It is no accident that the golden age of modern medicine and drug discovery, from 1900 to 1950, was the period when science was not yet disconnected from nature, when scientists tilled the soil, sharpened their gifts of observation of nature and the human body, and were in touch with the natural environment. They derived penicillin from fungus (1929–1940), streptomycin from a chicken's throat (1944), chloramphenicol from the soil (1947), chlortetracycline and cephalosporin from the soil (1948), neomycin from the earth (1949), oxytetracycline from farm soil (1950), insulin hormone from the pancreas (1914), cortisone and streptomycin from naturally occurring compounds (1949). After many years of wandering in the wilderness of genetic engineering, genetic screening and gene therapy costing billions of dollars in research with little or nothing to show for it, modern science is now looking back towards the African bush. After billions of dollars in cancer research with no sign of a solution in sight, science is beginning to wonder if the solution is not actually closer again to nature as well as to humanity.

Gradually, the modern world is beginning to recover the true meaning of research. *Re-search*: to search for something that was once known but forgotten, to look again for what is missing. In fact, there is a connection between *re-search* and *re-ligion*, from the Latin word *re-ligare* (to re-bind, re-unite, re-connect with a higher power). True scientists are spiritual by nature. Science does not and cannot create. Science only tries to re-discover, to re-fine, to re-interpret, re-design, re-confirm and *re-search* what is already there in nature. Call it what you want – chemistry, physics, agronomy, botany, microbiology, medical science, biology, anatomy, engineering, biochemistry, psychology, sociology, anthropology, economics, it still boils down to the same thing: *Nature.*

ACIRD: linking research to innovation in Africa

The Africa Centre for Integral research and Development (ACIRD), then, is passionate about research, both processually and also substantively, that leads to social, if not also technological, innovation in Africa. There are first in Africa and other parts of the world brilliant individuals who have done marvellous research work and have produced excellent academic works in various fields of social research. Most of these individual researchers often die unknown, some are frustrated due to lack of a platform to give flesh to their theories, while some simply lose interest in academic work and focus on "more important things". African intellectuals, on the one hand, in diverse fields do research for the sake of research: research that contributes little or nothing to individual, and communal, organizational and societal development. Moreover, and on the other hand, they fail to document, disseminate or indeed systematically critique, what African practitioners, as exemplars of "best practice", in the public, private, civic and environmental arenas, have achieved. The result is that their research works end in beautifully, or not so beautifully, written dissertations and publications that gather dust in libraries.

What, then, are the aims and objectives, and the proposed activities, of ACIRD, as a research academy so to speak, in association with Ibadan University's Institute for African Studies and Trans4m's Centre for Integral Development, thereby taking on from where Chancellor Williams in Constituting the South, if not also Ibrahim Abouleish and Heliopolis University for Sustainable Development in Egypt, have left off?

Aims and objectives

Overall aims:

- Develop distinct Afrocentric research methods and research method-ology interdependent with, rather than dependent upon, the dominant Eurocentric system.
- Research and develop the theory of communitalism, at both macro and micro levels, as the African antidote to the imbalances of rampant capitalism, relevant to particular societies and enterprises both within Africa and without.

Specific objectives:

- Giving voice to the oft-neglected voices from the peripheries, which account for 80 per cent of the world's population.
- Revising the past and interpreting it in our own southern voice and metaphors as against the overly westernized narratives.
- Charting a path through research to a sustainable socio-economic and political liberation of Africa, duly documented and disseminated, operating at both micro and macro levels.
- Developing the concept of cognitive justice as key to social, economic, political, mental and moral liberation of Africa.

Activities:

- Publication of research work in the natural, medical and social sciences.
- Community activation through the association of Ewu Development and Educational Association, an independent, self-governing body owned by the local community in Ewu.

- Development and ongoing evolution of the theory of communitalism.
- Dissemination of integral research knowledge through the Trans4m/ Routledge book series on Innovation and Transformation as well as Integral Green Economies and Societies.
- Annual/bi-annual international conferences on African knowledge systems.

Conclusion

The world has failed to appreciate the zeal and passion with which the African elite pursued the myth of the independent nation-state in the twentieth century. In the twenty-first century, a knowledge-driven sustainable development in Africa, for Adodo, must be pursued more forcefully to narrow the growing knowledge divide, which will not be achieved in large parts of Africa without a profound reform of such knowledge.

African societies must seriously take up the tremendous knowledge challenges they face. They must invest massively in knowledge to improve the social soil and environment on which it grows, keep abreast of knowledge development, set in motion dynamic knowledge-creating processes, reduce knowledge deficits, free knowledge from impurities, strengthen knowledge infrastructures and institutions, fight knowledge obsolescence and increase knowledge performance. They must embark on a new adventure of knowledge leading to integral knowledge-led sustainable development.

ACIRD has taken up the challenge, in association with African others, locally and regionally, most specifically with Centers of Integral Development in Zimbabwe (Pundutso), and South Africa (AFlead) and Sekem's Centre for Social Innovation in Egypt, together with Trans4m globally, of filling part of the knowledge deficit prevalent in Africa. The journey to a true *Pax Africana* has begun. Along the way *Pax Natura is embedded in nature and community – southern humanism; Pax Spiritus becomes a sanctuary embodying culture and spirituality – eastern holism; Pax Scientia is a university of social science and technology – northern rationalism; Pax Economia is a laboratory for economy and enterprise – western pragmatism; and each form of genealogy ultimately complements the other.*

In the final analysis though, and to the extent that Pax Africana gains functional as well as structural ground, more purposefully, it will need to clearly differentiate between communitalism, functionally, and genealogy, structurally. We shall consider the above, genealogically in more reasoned and realizable depth, in Chapter 9, but before that we now turn from the relational path to the path of renewal, and thereby to our *Social Ecology*, emerging in Zimbabwe.

References

Adodo, A. (2017) *Communitalism: Towards Pax Afrikana.* Abingdon: Routledge.

Lessem, R. and Schieffer, A. (2010) *Integral Research and Innovation: Transforming Enterprise and Society.* Abingdon: Routledge.

Lessem, R. *et al.* (2013) *Integral Dynamics: Cultural Dynamics, Political Economy and the Future of the University.* Abingdon: Routledge.

5 Social ecology

Integral Green Zimbabwe
African phoenix rising

Summary of chapter:

1 research replaces "I am because I have power" with "*I am because we are*";
2 connecting *spirit, rhythm and creativity*;
3 such linkages lead to new *meaning, motif, ethos, mode, function, method, form*;
4 this leads to the *ecological rethinking of leadership, knowledge and agriculture–industry–information technology* as problems are tackled contextually;
5 this culminates in an African phoenix that rises, embodied in *decoloniality*.

Introduction: a phoenix rising

Integral Green Zimbabwe

The same Martin Large whom we cited in Chapter 2 in the context of Sekem, introducing his recent work on *Commonwealth*, previously wrote a book on social ecology (1981), which anticipated both the innovation driven institutional Research, functionally, if not also the institutional genealogy, structurally, that is central to our *CARE* and CARE respectively. In fact, such an approach, in significant part, has been specifically anticipated by our research community in Zimbabwe over the past decade.

For Dr Elizabeth Sarudzai Mamukwa, lead editor of our recent book *Integral Green Zimbabwe: An African Phoenix Rising* (Mamukwa *et al.*, 2014) and a graduate of our Trans4m/Da Vinci PhD program, the innovation driven institutional research is to be carried out, and further emerge, through their *Pundutso* (meaning advancement or transformation in the local Shona language) *Centre for Integral Development*. This could potentially, if not yet actually, arise in conjunction with research institutes in Zimbabwe (Amakhosi Theatre), South Africa (Mafeje Research Institute),

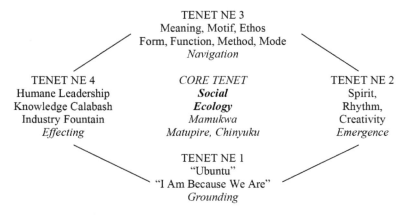

Figure 5.1 Institutional research renewal: emergent tenets.

North America (Boyer College, Philadelphia) and Europe (Trans4m, Geneva), altogether, in Zimbabwe, involving specific communities and organizations in solving given societal problems.

Such innovation driven research, as yet only partially institutionalized, has been inspired by both the gifts and the capacities of the PhD research community, and also by the economic and social ills that bedevilled Zimbabwe, particularly between 2004 and now in 2016, as was indeed the case for Mondragon (see Chapter 10), in the Basque country, emerging from the horrors of the Spanish Civil War. *The question thereby addressed is, how may we* (Mamukwa, *et al.*, 2014) *respond as a country, as an industry, as communities, as organizations and as individuals to burning issues that have resulted in a greater part of the population sinking into abject poverty?* There are few jobs for the children to take up; the granaries do not have enough stocks to feed the people; while the majority of companies have closed, those factories and companies still limping along have lost critical skills; and the family structure has been split, with one parent taking up a job in the Diaspora, to mention just a few of the challenges we faced. So how might we further emerge, by way of innovation driven, institutionalized research, along a path of African renewal?

Renewing a nation: the Zimbabwean phoenix is rising

The need for decoloniality

Zimbabwean-born University of South Africa-based Professor Ndlovu-Gatsheni, Head of the Archie Mafeje Research Institute for Applied

Social Research, part of the University of South Africa, embarks on a self-criticism drive (as an African and a Zimbabwean) where he first reflects on the issue of coloniality, whereby perhaps as Africans we continue to be our own colonizers (Ndlovu-Gatsheni, 2013). Well after independence, he contends, we continue to maintain the same institutions of colonization in the same way our colonizers used them. He terms this "coloniality", and suggests that, *for the Zimbabwean Phoenix to rise from the ashes, a process of "decoloniality" needs to take place.* For us this involves CARE generally, and innovation driven institutionalized Research specifically.

Ndlovu-Gatsheni asserts that Southern Africans may counter coloniality by influencing such institutions to rather develop knowledge for Africa as opposed to acting as care-takers to archaic colonial machinery. He further discusses the agony and violence in Africa, which he identifies as a struggle over limited resources. Relationally and developmentally, then, one way of addressing this violence is to increase those capacities that are in our power to increase, and *seek to replace the ethos of "I conquer therefore I am" with the ubuntu/unhu one of "I am because we are".*

Table 5.1 African phoenix rising

Innovation driven institutionalized research: relational path Integral Zimbabwe: leadership, knowledge and industry ecology African phoenix rising

- *Communal attributes*: Grounding – Constituting Africa, Sekem Commonwealth, European Trinity; Emergence – social research paradigm, *social ecology*, integral development; Navigation – communitalism, integral university, reinventing knowledge; Effect – social economy, knowledge creation, solidarity economy.
- *Integrator role:* research institute, e.g. *Gatsheni Ndlovu, Archie Mafeje Research Institute; Welsh-Asante, Boyer College of Music & Dance; Pundutso Centre for Integral Development.*
- *Research function*: scholarship, research and knowledge creation on *Integral Zimbabwe*.
- *Navigating knowledge creation*: such research replaces "I am because I have power" with *"I am because we are"*; connecting *spirit, rhythm and creativity*; such interactive linkages lead to new *meaning, motif, ethos, mode, function, method and form*; this gives direction to research, ultimately leading to the *ecological rethinking of leadership, knowledge and industry*; problems are tackled contextually, drawing on alternative knowledge systems: *Ubuntu-Unhu-Botho* (humane leadership), *Denhe re Ruzivo* (calabash of knowledge) and *Chitubu cheraramiso mumabasa* (industrial fountain) complementing the other, culminating in an African phoenix that rises, embodied in *decoloniality*.

Drawing on the social sciences and the humanities

A living example of such an approach is the Chinyika case, where people in rural Zimbabwe who had been on the verge of starvation transformed their area into a land of plenty where today, as of 2016, up to 300,000 people, in the process of rediscovering who they were as Africans, are now as a result well fed and there is a robust food security strategy in place (Lessem *et al.*, 2013). This in itself is a challenge to coloniality, as Zimbabweans in and around Chinyika have come up with workable local–global strategies of creating knowledge for Africa. Not only have they challenged the *coloniality of being* by grounding themselves in their African-ness, but they have attacked the *coloniality of knowledge* by creating knowledge for Africa, as we shall see.

Such knowledge, promoted by innovation driven institutional research (see for example such research institutions as Trans4m Centre for Integral Development in Geneva, Amakhosi Theatre in Zimbabwe, and Temple University's Boyer College of Music and Dance in Philadelphia, cited below) spans the social sciences (anthropology, sociology, psychology, economics and management) and the humanities (history, philosophy, theatre and dance) as *integral realms*. In what follows, we subscribe to the overall logic of that integral enterprise (Lessem and Schieffer, 2009), from community building to sustainable development, as per overall social ecology, functionally if not also structurally.

Community Activation: community building

Community Activation (see our first volume, *Community Activation for Integral Development*), for us, then, constitutes the starting point for a healthy society and economy, in Zimbabwe if not in Africa as a whole. For Chinyika-oriented Dr Chidara Muchineripi and Dr Steve Kada specifically, who participated in our Trans4m/Da Vinci Institute PhD program as well as a previous project-based Masters of ours, as indeed for Ndlovu-Gatsheni generally, the starting point was the trauma of colonization, which had the effect of upsetting the African ecology when foreign methods of farming and crops were introduced by the colonizers. The end result was that the people began to starve in Chinyika. The exogenous crops could not survive the droughts.

In the process of changing the face of Chinyika, traditional women (see Chapter 1 on *Constituting Africa*) were elevated to positions of leadership epitomized by the formidable, and at the same time humble, coordinator of the community council, Mai Mlambo. The women of Chinyika had, through the relational research path spearheaded by Muchineripi and Kada, combined their new leadership role with their traditional ones of cooking and singing to make the work lighter. In the process of going back to their communal roots, genealogically so to speak (see Chapter 8), the people of Chinyika also reverted back to the traditional technology of storing finger millet in sealed granaries, which has gone a long way towards safeguarding their food security.

Awakening integral consciousness: conscious evolution

Theatre for community activation

While Muchineripi and Kada came to the realization, almost now a decade ago while on our Masters program in Social and Economic Transformation, that they could activate their Chinyika community to take charge of their situation, thereby building up towards self-sufficiency, for Cont Mhlanga, spanning many years before this time, a spiritual calling had in fact occupied his entire adult life (Mamukwa *et al.*, 2014). Mhlanga had then, at Amakhosi Theatre in Bulawayo, worked at teaching and encouraging young artists not only to become good at their art but also to use their artistic talent to make a living. As such, he seeded what we term a culture-based developmental society and economy, generally (see *Awakening Integral Consciousness*), if not also specifically a sanctuary for local artists to both conserve and grow their talents. He has then, over two decades, catalyzed young people to believe in themselves, both artistically and enterprise wise.

As such, a large number of successful Zimbabwean artists have passed through his "academy". The role that Mhlanga has played has greatly contributed to keeping young people off the streets, and to giving an opportunity to serious artists to start and pursue their careers. Over and above this, *he has also activated the adult community in a bid to get them to take charge of their situation through an action research program he termed Theatre for Community Action (TCA)*, thereby combining theatre studies, community development, and business studies. Through the TCA methodology he activated the community to work through their problems, such as HIV/AIDS, gender equality and others.

Most important of all, though, Mhlanga, through his Amakhosi Theatre, raised the consciousness of young people as well as that of the community as a whole, and gave them hope, thereby awakening a developmental consciousness, in the individual, in conjunction with community and society, mediated through local as well as global culture and spirituality.

We now turn from theatre to dance. In the process we turn from a theatre for community action, so to speak, to an aesthetic process underlying an innovation driven approach to institutionalized research, as we shall see.

Nzuri as a pan-African aesthetic

African–American choreographer and academic Kariamu Welsh-Asante, based at Temple University's Boyer College of Music and Dance in Philadelphia, and one-time director of Zimbabwe's National Dance Company in the early 1980s, soon after independence, focuses on *Nzuri* as a pan-African aesthetic (Welsh-Asante, 1993). Such Nzuri sources are ntuonic (that is, each source is a unit of *Ntu*, the life force or vital energy referred to in Chapter 3). More specifically *Nzuri* is infused with the *Ntu*- life force, the infinite cosmological energy that permeates all beings and all things. *Ntu* joins everything and flows through everything. The three units of *Nzuri* are:

- *Spirit*: the first manifestation of *Ntu*, as is most clearly linked to *Kra* or the soul. Indeed, this soul force is the metaphysical experience of humans and as such it provides an inner world of ideas, thoughts and emotions.
- *Rhythm*: rhythm here is integral to the life force of every African. Unsurprisingly, in this light and for example, entrepreneurship, and leadership, lose their western gloss, and assume rather African aesthetic life-giving proportions.
- *Creativity*: generally, creativity is indeed an expansive concept, one that enlarges and envisions the world as a specific society as well as the artist him/herself. Specifically it is one of the material manifestations of spirit and rhythm, the two preceding *sources*, both communally and individually affirming and serving both.

Nzuri entities

Nzuri, secondly, is constituted of pyramidal entities that are used in the production of an artistic manifestation, and could easily be related to business and management, politics or economics:

- *meaning*: significance of expression in relationship to individual and community.
- *motif*: use of symbols in artistic product that reflect a particular culture and heritage.
- *ethos*: quality of expression that exudes sprit.
- *mode*: manner in which artistic product is expressed.
- *function*: operative relationship of artistic product to individual and community.
- *method*: practical, physical and material means of realizing artistic product.
- *form*: status of artistic product in terms of structure, shape and composition.

Integral Nzuri principles

Principles, thirdly, are elements in the *Nzuri* model that transmit, affirm and respond to the artistic product. From our perspective these correspond with the release of GENE-ius (Grounding, Emergence, Navigating, Effect):

- *Oral Principle (Grounding)*: transmission of traditional artistic and *rhythmical* forms including storytelling, music, dance and literature.
- *Ashe Principle (Emergence)*: affirming tradition through reinforcement, reliance and enhancement, as well as overall immersion – *losing yourself* – in the artistic product.
- *Ehe Principle (Navigation)*: values expression, or *communication*, that comes from an individual that is contained and continued within the value parameters of society.
- *Nommo Principle (Effect)*: the manifestation of energy in all of its varied forms both spoken and unspoken, movement and gesticulation.

Innovation driven institutionalized research: knowledge creation

Integral ubuntu leadership ecology: Ubuntu–Unhu–Botho

So far most of the institutionalized research to which we have referred has drawn upon research institutions outside Zimbabwe, in South Africa (Archie Mafeje) and in the United States (Boyer College). We now move specifically to *Pundutso* in Zimbabwe, whose research has focused more on bringing solutions to the enterprise, through combining technological with more specifically social innovation.

Three mature researchers to begin with – Dr Passmore Matupire, founder of Kairos as a developmental consultancy, Dr Liz Mamukwa, now Human Resource Director of Liquid Telecom, and Dr Josh Chinyuku, as Managing Director of Astra Paints – worked together as a cooperative inquiry group on our PhD program in Integral Development, thereby becoming an emergent *Pundutso* Centre for Integral Development (Heron, 1996). Their aim, altogether, was to transform the way businesses are run in Zimbabwe, through developing a leadership, knowledge and industrial ecology, as three elements that have the potential to renew Zimbabwean manufacturing industry, while at the same time serving to evolve the relational, *ubuntu*-related research agenda.

Matupire set the tone by pointing to institutional and leadership failure. He introduced Scharmer and Kaufer's (2013) exogenous (US-based) assertion that the world is destructive at ecological, socio-economical and spiritual levels, emanating from a disconnect between self and nature. He then, in his *Ubuntu Integral Leadership* (2016), provided building blocks of indigenous theories and practices of leadership, *Ubuntu–Unhu–Botho*, as the grounding philosophy, striving for completeness through leading a balanced life, thereby acknowledging the interconnectedness of a community, where peace, harmony, dignity and compassion prevail. For a leader to be integral, he should first master himself and become a total African person who balances his life among family, ethics, career, education, culture, spirituality and health, as well as the south and east, north and west within.

Calabash of knowledge creation: knowledge ecology – Denhe re Ruzivo

Dr Liz Mamukwa took the industry story on from here and focused her attention on her organization. She concentrated her research on knowledge creation after observing that, when employees of her company left the organization, they took their skills with them, thereby creating a "destitute" enterprise. Using the metaphor of the calabash, she created a model that spoke to an African mode of transferring knowledge from one person to the other as well as promoting the creation of new knowledge.

Through *Denhe re Ruzivo* (Calabash of knowledge), Dr Mamukwa's cooperative inquiry group at her manufacturing company Turnall Holdings, with the help of *Pundutso*, explored the knowledge creation cycle (see *Awakening of Integral Consciousness*) of Nonaka and Takeuchi (1995), from which a more indigenous model was developed. While initially based on the four components of Socialization, Externalization, Combination and Internalization as prescribed by Nonaka, functionally, Dr Mamukwa added some critical Afrocentric tenets to it, though not yet further evolving the hypertext structure – knowledge base, bureaucratic system, project layer – of the knowledge creating company in her enterprise case (Nonaka and Takeuchi, 1995).

Such rhythm and maturity is therefore implied in the development of new knowledge. This brings us on to so-called "industry ecology".

Industry ecology: Chitubu Cheraramiso Mumabasa

Josh Chinyuku, having been a leading figure for many years in the Zimbabwean Chamber of Industries (CZI), broadened this industry base further by focusing on industry associations, as well as on industry and society. He identified the need for a social solution to solving industrial problems such as high costs of bringing imported raw materials into the country, shipping and logistic challenges, as well as high-import duties on imports. Such challenges incorporated working with local suppliers to develop substitute raw materials and packaging, and sharing this at sector, industry and enterprise level. Like that of Matupire and Mamukwa, Chinyuku's approach was grounded, in theory if not also in practice, in *Ubuntu/Unhu*. For Chinyuku, the critical factor for industrial companies to survive is that, rather than being exclusively in competition with one another, they also needed to work together, resulting in a mode of co-opetition rather than pure competition.

For Chinyuku, then, these models, again functionally more than structurally oriented, represent African rhythms, which enable the working together of the different entities. We now turn from Community Building, Conscious Evolution and Knowledge Creation, as per our *Integral Enterprise*, finally on to Sustainable Development, where we give insights into the works of Zimbabwean/US-based agronomist Allan Savory and St Vincent Secondary School-based educator and pedagogue Dr Mark Marombedza.

Transforming education, learning and enterprise: sustainable development

Holistic land management

Allan Savory, who founded the Savory Institute in New Mexico and the Centre for Holistic Management in Zimbabwe, shares the story of Dimbangombe Ranch, managed by his research institute – that is, the Africa Centre for Holistic Management – near Victoria Falls (Savory, 1999). In this ranch, desertification has been reversed by, among other initiatives, increasing the number of large grazing animals fourfold. The message that comes out loud and clear, from Savory's five decades of research, is that solutions to some of humanity's most complex problems are within reach. He reminds us, as Muchineripi did at the outset of our research and development, that agriculture plays a critical role in human life, yet humans tend to be careless about how we look after the land, hence contributing to land degradation and desertification. This desertification is a threat to humans and animals alike. Savory points out that it is possible to experience drought without any change in the rainfall patterns, because rains become less effective as a result of land degradation. That is the reason there is a drought at one end of the river and floods at the other.

Contrary to what we are told, Savory contends that over-resting land is the biggest cause of desertification. Livestock, then, can play the role of regenerating the land. He adds that communities fail because they do not adopt holistic, for us integral, ways of managing their situations.

The best solutions, however, are the ones that embrace science and tradition, indigenous and exogenous knowledge.

Education for sustainable development: Boka Rokutsvagurudza

Dr Mark Marombedza builds on Savory's argument in turning, as an educationalist, to permaculture, based at the St Vincent Secondary School in Ruwa. In Zimbabwe in particular the erratic electricity supply has resulted in a higher demand for firewood for cooking, resulting in the increased cutting of trees with no plan for replacement of those felled. Veldt fires have also been a menace. The results have included silted rivers, poor-quality water and poor soil sanitation, leading to propensity towards flooding. Marombedza then identified permaculture as a desirable solution to some of these problems, as it is an integral land use design, drawing in particular on examples from neighbouring Malawi. The school successfully reclaimed its grounds through permaculture design, prompting the then Minister of Education to launch a pilot Schools and Colleges Permaculture Programme (SCOPE) in 18 schools. More recently, Marombedza has picked this up with his research group, St Vincent *Boka Rokutsvagurudza*, by planting indigenous trees and herbal plants for medicinal purposes at Makumbi Mission.

Conclusion: the Zimbabwean eagle, flying in the sky

If we revisit our overall, institutionalized research agenda, we have argued that *such research replaces "I am because I have power" with "I am because we are", connecting spirit, rhythm and creativity; such interactive linkages lead to new meaning, motif, ethos, mode, function, method and form; this gives direction to research, ultimately leading to the ecological rethinking of leadership, knowledge and agriculture–industry–information technology; problems are tackled contextually – Ubuntu–Unhu–Botho (humane-ness), Denhe re Ruzivo (Calabash of knowledge) and Chitubu cheraramiso mumabasa (industrial fountain) complementing the other, culminating in an African phoenix that rises and is embodied in decoloniality.*

However, for all of this to become a reality, the respective research institutions involved, combined with the range of disciplines encompassed in the social sciences and humanities, would need to become reciprocally engaged, specifically structurally, in an Inter-institutional Genealogy that serves to further evolve, and indeed navigate, the Social Ecology. With a view indeed to this, we now pursue such emergence, on the path of reasoned realization, via our own Trans4m Centre for Integral Development.

References

Heron, J. (1996) *Co-operative Inquiry: Research into the Human Condition.* London: Sage.

Large, M. (1981) *Social Ecology: Exploring Post-Industrial Society.* Stroud: Hawthorne.

Lessem, R. and Schieffer, A. (2009) *Transformation Management: Toward the Integral Enterprise.* Abingdon: Routledge.

Lessem, R., Muchineripi, P. and Kada, S. (2013) *Integral Community: Political Economy to Social Commons.* Abingdon: Routledge.

Mamukwa, E., Lessem, R. and Schieffer, A. (2014) *Integral Green Zimbabwe: An African Phoenix Rising.* Abingdon: Routledge.

Matupire, P. (2016) *Ubuntu Integral Leadership.* Abingdon: Routledge.

Ndlovu-Gatsheni, S. (2013) *Empire, Global Coloniality and African Subjectivity.* New York: Berghahn.

Nonaka, I. and Takeuchi, H. (1995) *The Knowledge Creating Company: How Japanese Companies Create the Dynamics of Innovation.* New York: Oxford University Press.

Savory, A. (1999) *Holistic Management: A New Framework for Decision Making.* Washington DC: Island Press.

Sharmer, O. and Kaufer, K. (2013) *Leading from the Emerging Future.* San Francisco, CA: Berrett-Koehler.

Welsh-Asante, K. (ed.) (1993) *The African Aesthetic: Keeper of the Traditions.* Westport, CT: Praeger.

6 Integral development

Creating ecosystems, renewing self, organization and society

Regenerating knowledge, actualizing development

Summary of chapter:

1 centre – catalyzing integral development;
2 community – co-creating ecosystems, community activation;
3 culture – renewing self, organization and society, awakening consciousness;
4 innovation – regenerating knowledge, institutionalized research;
5 impact – actualizing development, embodying development.

Introduction

We now turn, emergent wise on the path of reasoned realization, to Trans4m's Centre for Integral Development, lodged in Geneva–Hotonnes, duly in the European "north-west". Our Trans4mative focus on innovation driven institutionalized Research as such, hitherto in Nigeria and Zimbabwe, from a respectively relational and renewal perspective, is also

Figure 6.1 Trans4m: catalyzing integral development.

reflected (see next volume, *Embodying Integral Development*) in Slovenia, now altogether pursuing our four research paths, relation and renewal, and most especially reason and realization. As such, in this chapter, we turn to Trans4m (2016) itself – that is, to our overall approach to *Integral Development* in that light. In the process we shall also be incorporating our GENE and our CARE (see below) as a whole.

We start then with our CARE Centre.

CARE: centre and purpose – catalyzing integral development

Trans4m is a passionate enabler of individual and collective development, invariably lodged within a particular society. We address the burning issues of our time, releasing individual and collective genius.

Headquartered in Geneva, Switzerland, and Hotonnes, France, the Trans4m movement works through its Fellows, Integral Centers and Partner Organisations literally on all continents. (Trans4m, 2016)

At its core, Trans4m is a development catalyst of a new integral theory and practice, supporting particular individuals and organizations, communities and societies to engage reciprocally in carefully designed developmental processes, in order to develop their full potential and to contribute, in a sustainable and life-affirming way, to the development of local and global nature and humanity.

Table 6.1 Trans4m Centre for Integral Development

Innovation driven institutionalized research: relational path Centre for Integral Development GENE and CARE

- *Communal attributes*: Grounding – Constituting Africa, Sekem Commonwealth, European Compass; Emergence – social research paradigm, social ecology, *Integral Development*; Navigation – communitalism, integral university, institutional genealogy; Effect – social economy, knowledge creation, solidarity economy.
- *Integrator role*: research institute, e.g. **Lessem, Schieffer and Trans4m Individual and Institutional Associates**.
- *Integral functioning*: **Purpose, Community, Culture, Innovation, Impact**.
- *Navigating integral development*: Centre/Purpose – *catalyzing integral development*; Community – *co-creating ecosystems*; Culture – *renewing self, organization and society*; Innovation – *regenerating knowledge*; Impact – *actualizing development*.

Trans4m sees itself as an integral response to a "world on fire" – a world that is facing massive socio-ecological–economic–spiritual imbalances that altogether threaten the very existence of people and planet. A local–global movement for integral development, Trans4m's locally and globally active agents of integral development, are committed to participate – together with their organizations and communities – in developing and applying holistic solutions for locally burning issues, in culturally and societally relevant and resonant ways. Moreover, and in the process, we develop overall institutional ecologies, or genealogies (see Chapter 9 below), to accomplish this.

How then, more specifically, do we go about this? We start with community.

Community: co-creating ecosystems – learning community

The foundation of the Trans4m movement is its vibrant community of integral individual and institutional agents of transformation – passionately engaged in activating our particular selves, organizations, communities and societies to participate in the integral renewal of people and planet. Jointly, we are co-creating living innovation ecosystems – enabling sustainable, integral solutions to burning issues to be grounded locally, and to contribute globally. More specifically, in relation to each *community*, we see ourselves jointly as,

- *a contextualized platform for communal learning and development, enabling communities to reclaim their full problem-solving potential;*
- *recognizing communal stewards deeply immersing themselves in a particular natural and communal context, relating to other human beings and to nature;*
- *embodying the web of life representing interdependency, the circle of physical and human nature reflecting the oneness of their community.*

Trans4m was initially founded by Afro-European Ronnie Lessem and citizen of the world Alexander Schieffer, both having a business and economic background combined with a passion for culture and the psychology of consciousness. Trans4m, though, is not centred on one or a few leading personalities, but forms a living local–global institutional ecology, or indeed genealogy, that co-creatively gives birth to integral development, encompassing nature, culture, technology and economy in an all-round polity. Local nature, then, is our starting point. Inspired by nature's principles and by deep ecology, we conceive of integral development as co-evolutionary, interdependent, highly attuned processes that require ecosystemic, supportive environments to flourish.

It is on these principles that our key transformative processes – "CARE" and "GENE-ius" – are designed. While CARE stands for Community activation, Awakening integral consciousness, innovation driven Research and Embodying integral development, our recognition of GENE-ius involves, analogously, Grounding, Emergence, Navigation and Effect. The institutional container for both of these is a composite of Community, Sanctuary, University and Laboratory.

We saw in the previous chapter a prime example of such Communal learning and activation in the development of Chinyika, generally. In fact we, Trans4m, engage with such communities around the world – naturally and culturally, technologically and economically – and most specifically in Zimbabwe, South Africa and Nigeria in Africa; in Egypt, Jordan and Palestine in the Middle East; in India, Pakistan and Sri Lanka in the Near East; in UK, Germany and Slovenia in Europe; and in Brazil and Paraguay in the Americas. Such engagement is invariably a by-product of the undergraduate and postgraduate educational programs that we run, in partnership with universities in Africa and Europe.

We now turn from community to culture, from community activation to awakening integral consciousness, from local grounding to local–global emergence.

Culture: renewing self, organization, society – development sanctuary

Purposefully catalyzing the rich creative, spiritual and cultural diversity, inherent in our individual selves and in our collective organizations, communities and societies, is central to Trans4m's approach to the full release of our particular and universal human potential. It is for this reason that our movement's own growth is driven by a combination of, (a) enabling individual growth processes of agents of transformation, (b) enhancing the development of organizations and communities with which they are associated, (c) co-evolving integral centres, and institutional ecologies, that act as local agencies for cultural and societal renewal, as well as, (d) co-engaging with an entire society drawing on its unique cultural potential.

As such, and for us, we function as a *developmental* sanctuary, whereby:

- *individual and collective learning and consciousness raising serve to renew cultural and spiritual sources of organization, community, society;*
- *a development catalyst is able to engage with cultural/spiritual dynamics of a particular entity/place, able to co-evolve with individual/ institutional others;*

- *a spiral of conscious co-evolution represents the regeneration and renewal of the spirit, culture and consciousness of a person/enterprise/ place.*

Of primary importance is the actualization of new integral realities – each one of us in our particular local contexts, societies and cultures – thereby transcending the burning issues humanity is facing towards positive, wholesome futures.

It is in this spirit, that Trans4m's originating centre is hosted in a place that is seeking to practically embody all "Integral Worlds". Called "Home for Humanity", Trans4m's main base in the French Jura Mountains near Geneva, is,

- a *Community-in-Nature*: where relationships to self, others and nature can be restored, and where the interdependent fabric of our community is continuously expanded and strengthened;
- an *Earth Sanctuary*: where the soul of a person feels nourished, and the soulful quality of his or her community and society is recognized, and where the cultures of our world are mutually enriched, side by side;
- a *Sanctified Academy-and-Laboratory*: where reflection, knowledge creation and action learning take place, duly informed by such soulful awareness, and where new ideas are developed into concepts and processes; where new integral practice can be piloted and strengthened, with our local and global community.

For example, take the case of the Alpine region of Solčavsko in Slovenia, and that of Marko Slapnik, the guardian of Center Rinka therein. This case demonstrates how a commitment to nature and tradition as its moral core, and the alignment of the local population under common goals released the integral development potential of an entire region. In this process, and as part of his own awakening of integral consciousness, Slapnik was instrumental in the institutionalization of its development approach in the form of a local development centre, Center Rinka.

Working together with the Slovenian Citizen Initiative for an Integral Green Economy and Society, incorporating nature, culture, technology and economy, further helped Solčavsko not only to explain its own unique development model, but also to share it increasingly with the wider region and society as a whole. Study Circles in that context, as a national project, turned out to be a significant development tool in Slovenian rural areas.

We now turn from community and sanctuary, community activation and the awakening of integral consciousness, to our Trans4m means of navigation, innovation driven, institutionalized research.

Innovation: regenerating knowledge – research academy

Catalyzing integral development requires the continuous regeneration of knowledge. We understand social knowledge as a "living phenomenon"; and in order to be relevant to the ever-changing social realities and burning issues humanity is confronted with, it has to be continuously renewed. This, however, needs to take place in locally relevant ways, contributing to and building on the particular nature and culture of each context, while at the same time being in resonance with society as a whole and with the world. This is for us another crucial facet of being "integral". Our Integral Worlds theory and our growing body of integral knowledge, developed by the Trans4m movement, is responding to this challenge, underlying our approach to integral Innovation, in association with knowledge creating others, as a research university:

- *scholarship, research and knowledge creation aims – in conjunction with the other genealogical entities – for social innovation;*
- *social researcher-and-innovators as such have conceptual and analytical ability, are able to share knowledge in a group, are able to deal with complexity;*
- *a resulting grid of knowledge representing intelligent, structure-seeking and organizing processes of knowledge creation appears across recognized disciplines.*

Moreover, for Trans4m, the four research paths – relational and renewal, reason and realization – are matched by equivalent, altogether integral, economic systems and enterprise functions. Economically, then, a "southern" natural and communal realm promotes a "Self-Sufficient community-based Economy"; an "eastern" cultural and spiritual realm promotes a "Developmental culture-based Economy"; a "northern" scientific and technological realm promotes a "Social knowledge-based Economy"; a "western" realm was promoted in the past through a neo-liberal market economy, but below the surface we can recognize the gradual emergence of what we called a "Living life-based Economy". The same goes for an integral enterprise, whereby as per the,

- *South*: we reground the enterprise and its products and services in nature and community, also in societal needs, thereby promoting "Community Building".
- *East*: we re-link the enterprise's evolution to its own cultural and spiritual foundations and to those of its surrounding society, thereby tapping into its creative resources and initiating a process of "Conscious Evolution".

- *North*: we rebuild and design organizational structures and processes based on developmental needs and co-evolutionary processes, thereby transforming technocratic operations to "Knowledge Creation".
- *West*: we redefine the role of finance within the organization as a supportive one to all other functions, and redesign it in such a way that it supports the overall "Sustainable Development" of the organization and society.
- *Centre*: the role of the centre is an inspiring, coordinating and overall transformational one. Strategy like leadership ceases to be implemented top-down by a governance unit on top of the hierarchy, but is seen rather as a central process of "Strategic Renewal", or of "organizational Renewal".

Specifically to operationalize such integral research, we turn to *Impact*.

Impact: actualizing development – social laboratory

Social innovation

Based on its Integral Worlds approach, Trans4m has developed, in actuality as well as in prospect, a set of integral processes and products. The processes pertain, in turn, to our composite CARE, that is, *Community activation* via community circles in situ, around the world; *Awakening integral consciousness* via a developmental sanctuary based in Hotonnes, France; *innovation driven institutionalized Research* aligned selective educational institutions; and finally *Embodying integral development* in self and community, organization and society, in fertile institutional ground, that is in integral enterprises and societies.

To the extent that such a laboratory fosters social innovation, it becomes,

- *a focal point for creative experimentation or a conducive space in which new social and economic practices can be conceived of, tested and implemented;*
- *home ground for a learning facilitator able to team up with others, to translate knowledge into capacities, having strong project management skills;*
- *focused, goal-oriented, co-creative, resulting in the active build-up of new infrastructure and institutions.*

Our process of Embodying integral development as a whole, then, is twofold: initially we developed a PhD/PHD in Integral Development. While the PhD, accredited by the Da Vinci Institute, applies to individual development, through integral research and innovation, this is amplified through the PHD – Process of Holistic Development – involving the individual together with his or her enterprise and/or community. Subsequently we developed an equivalent undergraduate program, accredited by St Gallen University, again in integral development, with a similarly complementary individual/collective orientation.

The most evolved version of the PhD/PHD currently, is that being taken with Manar al Nimer, Vice President of Medlabs Consultancy in Jordan, and the Medlabs group of laboratories, in the Middle East, as a whole. The complementary focus on this PHD is upon revitalizing the moral core of the company, on the one hand, and building an integral Medlabs enterprise, on the other.

Prospectively, and in addition, there are two prospects of such a PhD/PHD that have been initiated. The first one is in South Africa, with AFlead (African local economic assisted development), as a PHD, in conjunction with its CEO Dr Emil Nothnagel, as a PhD; the second is Providence Human Capital in Zimbabwe, as a PHD, together with its CEO Chipo Ndudzo, as a PhD. Whereas in the first case the PHD focus is on developing a Centre for Integral Development, in the second one it is on becoming an integral enterprise.

Conclusion

In the final analysis, our reason for being, as Trans4m, is encapsulated in our centre/purpose – *catalyzing integral development* as a whole; our focus on community – *co-creating ecosystems*; community activation; our orientation towards culture and consciousness; *renewing self, organization and society*; awakening consciousness; our focus on social innovation – *regenerating knowledge*; institutionalized research; and ultimately on social and economic impact – *actualizing development* and embodying development.

When it comes to *activating community*, indeed there are many agencies engaged with this, but most are focused on economy over ecology, and few if any are engaged in cultural, as well as ecological, technological and enterprise renewal. Moreover, as far as *awakening consciousness* is concerned, the overwhelming emphasis is on "individual" as opposed to collective consciousness, of a community, organization or whole society. Moving thereafter onto innovation, *social innovation* lags far behind its technological equivalent, and though it is becoming a bit of a buzzword today, not many take it really seriously. So we are left, finally, to finding ways and means of building all of the above elements into, and over and above, individual learning, while doing our best, at the same time, to advance the overall cause of individual and communal, organizational and societal, development, in a particular society. We now turn from an emergent Trans4m, and our budding integral development, to navigation via integral research, the would-be integral academy, and to our reinvention of knowledge, to take the Trans4m story emancipatory wise on.

Reference

Trans4m (2016) www.trans-4-m.com (accessed December 2016).

Part III

Navigation of institutionalized research

7 Integral research paradigm
Technological/social innovation
Integral research perspective

Summary of chapter:

1   the quest for social innovation – pursuing a relational orientation;
2   uncovering why social innovation falls behind technological innovation;
3   individual, analytic method into societal transformative methodology;
4   there is a need to institutionalize social research and innovation.

Introduction: quest for social innovation – a relational orientation

Beyond the innovation buzzword

Despite first, grounding wise, our *Constituting of the South*, the *Sekem Commonwealth* and the classical *European Trinity*, and second, emergent wise, co-evolving *Communitalism* in Nigeria, a *Social Ecology* in Zimbabwe and our own *Trans4m Centre for Integral Development* in France, the conventional economic (neo-liberal) and political (democratic–autocratic) wisdom still overshadows what we have together accomplished so far. Why, then, has there been a lack of such institutionalized social – as opposed to technological – research and innovation, *relationally, renewal wise and reasoned*, on a sustainable basis in the past, and how might we newly navigate in the future?

We begin this chapter, in initially addressing these questions, by introducing our new, integral research paradigm, then subsequently turning to the prospect of an integral academy (Chapter 8) and culminating (Chapter 9) such navigation with a more thoroughgoing reinvention of knowledge.

Research and more particularly *innovation* in fact, as we see it (Lessem and Schieffer, 2010), is the supposed keynote of our emerging "knowledge society" (Luyckx Ghisi, 2008). Each enterprise is concerned with it and claims that it will soon be "out of the market" if it loses its power to innovate. Entire societies, governments and political parties, especially in the "developed" world, nail their colours to the innovation mast, and thereby claim to be doing everything in order to promote this. Even Team GB's recent (summer of 2016) notable success at the Rio Olympics, aside from clearly visible talent and lottery funding, was attributed to knowledgeable coaching, planning and sophisticated monitoring equipment. Governments, however, and indeed people in general, have little understanding of what "*social*" – as opposed to technological – and thereby especially *relational*, innovation, might actually mean, in a *particular society*. This, then, is the initial, what we have termed *functional* navigational *CARE* issue, with a view to institutionalizing social research, that we seek to *relationally* redress, building on what has come before (chapters 1–6), in Africa, in the Middle East, in Europe.

A particular society: beyond universalized technology

Our claim as such is not that we should abandon technological innovation, but that we tend to see such overall research and innovation in far too one-dimensional, invariably universalist if not also mono-disciplinary functional terms. There is more to *social* innovation than such a generalized approach. There is, or at least should be, *social* research and innovation lodged in, and drawing on the richly varied gifts and capacities of, a *particular* society. *It also thereby needs to be intimately connected with the social sciences generally, as well as the humanities – art and architecture, literature and theatre, dance and music, religion and philosophy of a community or society – particularly.* Imagine, by comparison, technological innovation taking place without prior knowledge of physics, chemistry, biology and/or mathematics, what we term the functional natural science equivalent of the above.

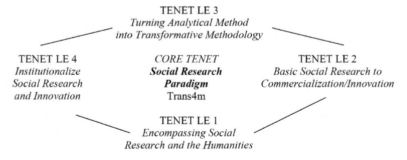

TENET LE 3
Turning Analytical Method
into Transformative Methodology

TENET LE 4   *CORE TENET*   TENET LE 2
Institutionalize   **Social Research**   *Basic Social Research to*
Social Research   **Paradigm**   *Commercialization/Innovation*
and Innovation   Trans4m

TENET LE 1
Encompassing Social
Research and the Humanities

Figure 7.1 Institutional relational research: navigation tenets.

Why social innovation falls behind technological innovation

Enterprise and university bereft of humanity

Yet when we ask many of our business or academic colleagues how they are advancing the lot of humankind generally, or that of Yemenis or Syrians specifically, through their corporate activities, on the one hand, or their "research" papers, on the other – if not also specifically their PhD theses – we usually get incredulous looks. There are of course exceptions to this rule, like those, at least to some extent, on our Trans4m/Da Vinci programs, as we shall see in the next chapter, but such exceptions are few and far between. Moreover, when we ask colleagues in the corporate sector how their research is contributing to resolving issues of social injustice, human poverty around the globe, the problem of world climate change, or, more recently, the global financial crisis, we get similarly blank looks. On the one hand, "That's all very well," the academics say, "our students just want to get a degree", or, "I have a PhD to complete." On the other hand, from business or management practitioners comes, "I have targets to meet", and "It's up to the government or the UN or NGOs or it's up to you people at the universities, to solve the world's problems, or Syria's, or Zimbabwe's, not us."

That is a big reason why, for us, "the world is on fire", and Syria, for example, is tragically burning! Thought and action, most especially that of a radical, transformative nature, while it might be the lot of a dedicated individual social researcher, is seldom institutionally met. Why is that?

Waking up to our research and innovation potential

First wake-up call: analysis without synthesis

Method and methodology are part of an integral whole

We start, functionally speaking, with research method/methodology. Take a look at the way social and economic, if not also psychological and cultural, research is typically positioned in universities, if not also within social research institutes, as well as corporations. Research "method", as conventionally conceived of, in the social sciences, conventionally ranging from quantitative to qualitative, is a form of universalized "data processing", drawn, for example, from census data, interviews, focus groups, statistically based polling, questionnaires or case studies.

Few researchers, as such, or indeed more especially research institutions, are aware of the fact that *research method and methodology are each a part of a more integral particular–universal whole*, thereby incorporated into

Table 7.1 Integral research paradigm

Innovation driven institutionalized research: relational path Institutionally reframes knowledge through innovative social science Contributes to integral knowledge creation in a particular society

- *Communal attributes*: <u>Grounding</u> – Constituting Africa, Sekem Commonwealth, European Trinity; <u>Emergence</u> – *social research paradigm*, social ecology, integral development; <u>Navigation</u> – communitalism, integral university, reinventing knowledge; <u>Effect</u> – social economy, knowledge creation, solidarity economy.
- *Integrator role*: researcher and innovator, e.g. *Trans4m*.
- *Research function*: scholarship, research and knowledge creation on *integral research and innovation*.
- *Navigating knowledge creation: the* **quest for social innovation** *– pursuing a relational orientation*; *uncovering* **why social innovation falls behind** *technological innovation due to lack of social "commercialization" as per innovation*; *turning from individual, analytic method into* **societal transformative methodology**; *there is a* **need to institutionalize** *social research and innovation.*

what we term our "integral research trajectory" or rhythm. This includes method (origination), methodology (foundation), critique (emancipation) and action (transformation), altogether in relation to one or other *particular research paths/reality/worldview*. In fact most researchers, within universities and without, engage with method or research as a technique, rather than with "methodology" as social philosophy – arising out of a particular worldview – without realizing the difference behind one (technique) and other (philosophy).

So it took us many long years of travelling through such a social and economic research desert, from Africa to Europe, on to American and Asia, indeed ultimately across four continents, before, as we shall see, several wake-up calls came along to transform our perspective. *The key that opened such a transformative door was our discovery that* invariably "northwestern" research paths could be reconceived as leading, *integrally* as we shall soon see, research wise from method (data-processing technique) on to research methodology (research paradigm) and beyond, and, innovation wise, from origination to transformation.

And yet research method and methodology fail to meet

There was, then, a *vast gulf between methodology (incorporating philosophy) and method (incorporating technique)* of which only the enlightened few had become aware. We had discovered that, among colleagues and students alike, *reference to method and methodology tended to be intertwined rather than clearly differentiated.* This mix of terms was replicated in much of the literature. The trouble is, then, that *methodology, or philosophy, remains disconnected from method or practicality, not to mention the fact that action research is all too often left out of the picture altogether, and hence innovation is curbed.* We now come to our second wake-up call.

Second wake-up call: lacking in integral worlds

Colonization of the minds

As our journey of discovery progressed, we came to the next revealing realization that, whereas *methodology was predominantly European* in origin, and *method was more likely to be American*, the *rest of the world virtually did not get a look in at all.* In other words, whether researchers, as students, came from South Africa or the Middle East, China or India, as well as Europe and the US, their research orientation would invariably be European or American. The same "research method" course would apply to practitioners, engaged with us in "research" projects from China or India, South Africa or the Arab world. Somehow that "north-western" predominance did not make sense to us. No wonder the world was on fire. Furthermore, the very fact that the philosophical "northern" Europeans predominated methodologically, and the practical "western" Americans prevailed method wise, meant that there was bound to be a gap in the mid-Atlantic!

Academe has given up its knowledge birthright

Furthermore, we found ourselves confused in between two knowledge domains with very different "rules of the game". For on the one hand, there was the field of applied enterprise where knowledge management, or indeed knowledge creation, had recently become the order of the day. Therein, as was the case for the "knowledge creating company", popularized by the two Japanese organizational sociologists Nonaka and Takeuchi (1995), it was the *norm to integrate diverse knowledge perspectives*, thereby originating or socializing (our southern), dialoguing or externalizing (our eastern), systematizing or combining (our northern) and practising or internalizing (our western). However, and on the other hand, *when it came to academic research in the social sciences, the norm was to specialize in one "western" research method or "northern" methodology.* So it seemed, as least in Nonaka's knowledge creating terms (see Chapter 11), one knowledge world predominated over the others, so that, in our terms, in research, there was a lack of worldly integrity.

Third wake-up call: need for functional and structural integration

Origination precedes foundation

Our third wake-up call had several connected parts to it, paving the way for social research-and-innovation that is ultimately integral, both in terms of worldviews (realities) and trajectory (rhythm).

First, then, having discovered that research methodology was indeed philosophy, we were duly uplifted, but too much so. Our feet had left the ground, so that we, and also our research students, were up in the clouds. So called "phenomenology" and "critical rationalism", "postmodernism" and "critical realism", for example, were truly revolutionary in nature and scope. However, there was a twist in the revolutionary tale. For these research philosophies were difficult for your everyday student, practitioner, or indeed researcher, to grasp, from the ground up. No wonder social innovation is all too often short changed. Moreover, because such research methodologies, or philosophies, were "studied" by individual researchers, in academe, they were not adopted by institutions or accessed by society at large. They were certainly far too difficult, if not esoteric, to be grasped by "real world" practitioners, so that their revolutionary influence was severely circumscribed.

Emancipation succeeds foundation

What we simultaneously discovered, moreover, with a little help from Australian research philosopher Norman Blaikie (2007), was that what he termed "classical" and "contemporary" research methodologies were qualitatively different from each other. Whereas the longstanding *classical* ones – empiricism and the like – were foundational, so to speak, the more contemporary *critical* ones – like "critical theory", so called, were indeed *emancipatory*. So we decided not only to differentiate method (origination) from methodology (foundation), but also critique (emancipation) from both of the other two. So the overall rhythm, or what we now termed a *research trajectory*, as indicated above, went from origination (grounding) to foundation (emergence) to emancipation (navigation). Moreover, as we evolved from origination (method) towards foundation (methodology) and emancipation (critique), so we assumed an ever deeper, and broader, societal reach, thereby becoming ever more trans-disciplinary, spanning our *integral realms*. However, although the emancipatory approaches were more radical and transformative in intent than what came before, they still were primarily means of reflection rather than action.

Emancipation on to transformative action

Kurt Lewin, who founded action research in the 1950s, and was himself a refugee to the UK from Nazi Germany, claimed that research in the social sciences lacked authenticity if it did not involve action, to test out the otherwise inauthentic theory (Lewin, 1999). Moreover, as we were soon to discover, there were four fundamentally different, albeit related, approaches to such action research: generic action research (AR), socio-technical design (STD), cooperative inquiry (CI) and participatory action research (PAR).

Lo and behold, we then concluded, each embodied, in particular, one or other of our *integral realities*: western *realization* (AR), northern *reason* (STD), eastern *renewal* (CI) and southern *relational* (PAR). At this transformative point, moreover, building upon this ultimately action research orientation, we have left the individual researcher way behind, and have entered the realms of communal, organizational and societal transformation, whereby the integrating of the individual, the institutional and the societal becomes for real. We now wanted to move from the research-and-innovation process, in the social sciences and humanities, towards its institutionalization.

Institutionalizing social innovation

What gets in the way of institution building?

Individual research predominates

Characteristically and ironically, "social" science research, conventionally led by universities, is individually oriented, while natural science research and development, typically conducted, and thereby institutionalized, within corporate or governmental research laboratories, is team-, if not also organizationally oriented. In fact, and first then, one of the major stumbling blocks to assimilating the wide range of research methods and methodologies to which we have alluded, is that there are too many for the individual mind to absorb. Indeed, not only does authentic social innovation require an initial method, an established methodology, a radical critique and ultimately transformative action – hence leading from research to innovation – but it also needs to be trans-disciplinary.

The closest we get to this, functionally for example, is with the composite "Area Studies" (Mirsepasse *et al.*, 2003), involving, say, China or the Middle East, instigated by the US government after the last war. In fact there may be inter-disciplinary research into this, but there is certainly no social innovation, as for example applied to developing particular societies.

Educational or research process bereft of institutional structure

In other words, in social research, culminating in thoroughgoing social innovation, not only are a multiplicity of disciplines – *integral realms* – necessarily involved, but there needs to be a wide range of research paths, each with a fully integral trajectory, and ultimately an institutional geneal-ogy to support this. In contrast, as is the "research" norm, social scientists, invariably working as individuals rather than as research teams, go for the lowest common denominator. While, first, they stick to a single dis-cipline, be it economics or psychology, second, each researcher adopts a single research method – for example, a questionnaire-based, survey approach to "data processing" – bereft of a research trajectory, and third, their research is normally either footloose and fancy free, or institutionally hidebound by academic bureaucracy.

This is even more the case in developing countries, where human and physical resources are especially scarce. In developed countries, in the social sciences, the alternative may be to plump for one particular methodology favoured by a university department, say phenomenology, preferably a combination of method (technique) and methodology (philos-ophy), such as so-called "interpretive phenomenological analysis" (IPA) in psychology (Smith *et al.*, 2009). The overall result, all too often, is such analytically based, individually oriented, mono-disciplinary focused research, bereft of any integral trajectory, conducted within a single pro-gram, rather than contained within an institutional structure. At best, there may be a research centre, so called, but it will invariably be dependent on the talent and charisma of an individual "guru" (more often than not "north-western", specifically American), such as the academic corporate strategist Michael Porter at Harvard Business School (ISC, 2016) or the development economist Jeffrey Sachs at Columbia University's Earth Institute (2016). The rest of the university, then, Harvard or Columbia, will carry on in the same old departmentalized way, while outside America and Europe, by and large, no such institutionalized social research with significant impact exists at all.

Absence of a composite research-and-innovation team-and-institution

As we have indicated, then, while in the typical, university department, in the social sciences or the humanities, the focus is on the researcher as an individual, this is absolutely not the case in the corporate R & D laboratory, in the natural sciences, where the focus is on the research and development team (see Chapter 9 on *Integral Innovation* from *Awakening Integral Consciousness*, my previous volume), if not a whole department, of perhaps thousands of researchers. As such, and in this latter case, whereas one of the team members, as a fundamental researcher, would be both multidisciplinary in orientation, and also inclined to span a full research trajectory, others, in the innovation team, would be more specialized in design, engineering, production or sales, while the research institution in itself will be part of an overall, interdependent organizational system (Kash, 1989), involving university, laboratory and overall research community, albeit less likely a sanctuary!

Yet, ironically, over centuries, we have pointed to individual social philosophers and scientists, ranging from Aristotle to St Thomas Aquinas, from John Locke to Adam Smith, and more recently from John Maynard Keynes to Milton Friedman, to address these issues. Indeed, and during the neo-liberal heyday of the past thirty years, the best, and perhaps only, example we have of a team of social researchers, indeed a whole innovation driven research institute, is the *Chicago School of Economics*. Sadly, though, in this case the results of such "neo-liberal" policies – as per the myopically "westernized Chicago Boys", where Friedman and his social scientific cronies were based – have often been disastrous. Yet, in the final analysis, they were never short of resources!

Towards research and development in the social sciences

The natural sciences then, on the one hand, as we have now seen, at least in the industrialized world, provides many good examples of trans-disciplinary teams, and fully fledged innovation driven corporate as well as governmental and indeed non-governmental research institutions, for example based on bio-chemistry, genetic engineering, astrophysics or electronics. On the other hand, when it comes to the social sciences, while there are such trans-disciplinary fields as social psychology, or cultural anthropology, as well as, historically at least, political economics, each of these tends to be dominated by the major discipline (psychology, anthropology and economics in turn).

We now are ready to review our overall argument in this *relational* chapter on social innovation.

Conclusion: towards a research-and-innovation trajectory

Technological innovation: fundamental research/commercialization

Technological innovation, aside from its trans-disciplinary orientation, also involves a "research and development trajectory", which goes roughly like this:

- *fundamental* research, say in mathematics, physics, chemistry, biology;
- *applied* research, for example in electronics, biotechnology, nano-technology or astrophysics;
- *development*, including product and process design and engineering;
- *commercialization*, including finance, operations, project management, marketing and sales.

Altogether, then, in a corporate context, we can talk about the trajectory of research *and* development, together with commercialization, leading ultimately to technological innovation. We are aware of no real articulated equivalent in the social sciences and humanities. Even the superb Japanese organizational sociologists Nonaka and Takeuchi (1995), as we shall see in Chapter 11, relate their knowledge creating company to technological inno-vation. Indeed, it is not even commonplace to talk of fundamental (basic or blue-sky) versus applied social research, never mind development and commercialization, in economics or sociology (social science), in history or fine arts (humanities). So what hope is there of all-round social innovation!

Social innovation: releasing GENE-ius

So we have had to invent what we call our research *trajectory*, as per our *integral rhythm*, for the social sciences, on the one hand, and our *institutional genealogy* (see Chapter 9) on the other. Unsurprisingly it follows the logic of our GENE in both cases – Grounding/community, Emerging/sanctuary, Navigating/university, Effecting/laboratory – because social research inevi-tably applies to a particular society, if not also to a particular organization.

Overall, then, and altogether as such, in the quest for social innovation, pursuing a relational orientation, there is a need to uncover why social inno-vation falls behind technological innovation, whereby individual, analytic method subsumes societal transformative methodology, and there is ulti-mately a need to institutionalize social research and innovation. We now turn from social – indeed integral – research as an activity and process, to a would-be integral academy, as an institutional structure, revealing both its possibilities and constraints, as such.

References

Blaikie, N. (2007) *Approaches to Social Inquiry: Advancing Knowledge*. Cambridge: Polity Press.

Earth Institute, Columbia University (2016) At http://www.earthinstitute.columbia.edu/ (accessed December 2016).

ISC (Institute for Strategy & Competitiveness), Harvard Business School (2016) About Michael Porter. At http://www.isc.hbs.edu/about-michael-porter/Pages/default.aspx (accessed December 2016).

Kash, D. (1989) *Perpetual Innovation: The New World of Competition*. New York: Basic Books.

Lessem, R. and Schieffer, A. (2010) *Integral Research and Innovation*. Abingdon: Routledge.

Lewin, K. (1999) *The Complete Social Scientist: A Kurt Lewin Reader*. Worcester, MA: American Psychological Association.

Luyckx Ghisi, M. (2008) *The Knowledge Society: The Breakthrough toward Genuine Sustainability*. Kerala: Stone Hill Foundation.

Mirsepassi, A., Basu, A. and Weaver, F., eds (2003) *Localizing Knowledge in a Global World: Recasting the Area Studies Debate*. Syracuse, NY: Syracuse University Press.

Nonaka, I. and Takeuchi, H. (1995) *The Knowledge Creating Company*. Oxford: Oxford University Press.

Smith, J., Flowers, P. and Larkin, M. (2009) *Interpretive Phenomenological Analysis: Theory, Method and Analysis*. London: Sage.

8 Integral academy

A developmental perspective

Summary of chapter:

1 the community academy serves to institutionalize community activation;
2 a developmental academy serves to awaken integral consciousness applied to enterprise, economy and development;
3 a research academy underlies innovation driven, institutionalized research;
4 an academy of life is one where integral development is fully embodied;
5 each form of academy ultimately complements the other.

Introduction: towards actualizing integral development

Diversity in unity

We now turn from the *relational* path of *social* research, and innovation, to the *renewal* of the academic institution that gives rise to it – that is, a would-be *integral academy*, whether at pre-, primary, secondary or tertiary educational levels. In our book *Integral Development: Realising the Transformative Potential of Individuals, Organizations and Societies* (Schieffer and Lessem, 2014), we thereby articulated what such an academy (at the time of writing, in 2013, referred to as a "university" before our thinking evolved in 2016) may be like. In this chapter, then, as an *emancipatory* design if not yet as a *realized* reality, we shall be embodying each element of functional *CARE* (in the next chapter we shall turn as well to structural CARE), respectively, within a type of academy function that best represents each one:

- a "*uni-que*" educational–developmental expression of an actualized developmental journey;
- "*uni-ting*" individual and communal, organizational and societal development;

- *"uni-versalizing"* development theory and practice through making it accessible for the world – though remaining in *"uni-on"* with its particular locale;
- thereby nurturing a world of *"uni-ty"* in *"di-versity"*, locally and globally.

Each unity-in-diversity, so to speak, actualizes the full potential of a particular element of CARE, and hence serves to contribute significantly to the realization of its core value. In that sense, each of the four Academy types introduced is also a reflection of the core characteristics of its respective realm. In Table 8.1 we show all four Academy types – applying to pre-school, school, university and research institute – in an overview.

A four-fold academy

Only one of the four functional types shows strong similarities with the conventional university or research institute, as we know it, though less so with a school, which is the *"northern"* Research Academy. However, we maintain that even such a Research University needs to be fundamentally reframed in order to fully actualize the *"northern"* realm and to authentically embody *innovation driven institutionalized (social) research –* as opposed to mere individual knowledge assimilation. Such *"reframing"* takes scholarship, research and knowledge creation out of their rather narrow, individual and abstract perspectives and links them, institutionally and collectively, to relevant communal and societal development needs and capacities. Indeed, this is what we are attempting to achieve through our emerging research centres, in integral banking, integral enterprise, integral community and integral development, albeit we are not quite there yet.

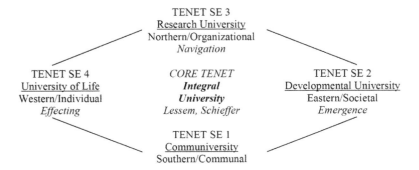

TENET SE 3
Research University
Northern/Organizational
Navigation

TENET SE 4
University of Life
Western/Individual
Effecting

CORE TENET
Integral
University
Lessem, Schieffer

TENET SE 2
Developmental University
Eastern/Societal
Emergence

TENET SE 1
Communiversity
Southern/Communal

Figure 8.1 Institutional reasoned research: emergent tenets.

Figure 8.2 Elements of the integral academy.

With this in mind, we now turn to each type to distil its major features, noting that every "academy" type, as a whole, embodies within it each respect element of CARE, as a part.

Table 8.1 The integral academy as a whole

Innovation driven institutionalized research: path of renewal Community academy, developmental academy, research academy, to academy of life Towards an integral academy
• *Communal attributes*: <u>Grounding</u> – Constituting Africa, Sekem Commonwealth, European Trinity; <u>Emergence</u> – social research paradigm, social ecology, integral development; <u>Navigation</u> – communitalism, *integral* *academy*, reinventing knowledge; <u>Effect</u> – social economy, knowledge creation, solidarity economy. • *Integrator role*: researcher and innovator, e.g. **Schieffer and Lessem**. • *Research function*: scholarship, research and knowledge creation on *integral* *academy*. • *Navigating knowledge creation*: such research is embodied in the *community* *academy* serving to institutionalize community activation; a *developmental* *academy* serving to awaken integral consciousness applied to enterprise, economy and development; a *research academy* underlying innovation driven, institutionalized social research; and an *academy of life* in which transformative education takes place, *each form of academy ultimately* *complementing the other.*

We start with the community academy.

Southern community academy: community activation

Village learning centres

The community academy, to begin with, is a quintessential expression of the "*southern*" realm of *nature and community*, as embodied in the Paxherbals/ Pax African case in Nigeria (see Chapter 1). It is a contextualized platform for communal learning and development. A community academy can be articulated as "*village learning centres*" or as community-based programs that draw purposefully on local, indigenous knowledge systems and build on the "*vitality*" of a particular place.

Healing communities

At the heart of the community academy is a "*healing component*" to restore the relational fabric within a community – required to release its participatory potential – and of the community to its natural environment. Chinyika's revitalization, as we saw in our previous volume on *Community activation* (Chapter 1), started with a community gathering on Chinyika rock, a place

Table 8.2 Learning community: community activation

Community academy: community activation Restores life in nature and community Contributes to healthy and participatory co-existence

• *Focus*: a contextualized platform for communal learning and development: communities reclaim their full problem-solving potential.
• *Required qualities of communal steward*:
  ○ ability to observe, empathize and care;
  ○ ability to face reality, to describe things as they are, not as one wants them to be;
  ○ ability to deeply immerse oneself in a particular natural and communal context;
  ○ ability to relate to other human beings;
  ○ ability to strongly relate to and care for nature.
• *Suggested symbol*: web of life representing interdependency of all life / the circle alludes to the original oneness underlying all of creation.

of great ancestral significance, and it focused, at least in its initial phase, almost exclusively on the reintroduction of finger millet as the core source of nourishment. The restoration of relationship in all its connotations – to oneself, among members of community, to other communities, to nature, to "*inner nature*" – is crucial to tap the developmental potential of a community and all its members. We now turn from the "southern" community academy, activating Community, to the "eastern" Developmental Academy, Awakening integral consciousness.

Eastern Developmental Academy: Awakening integral consciousness

A Developmental Academy, institutionally, and Awakening integral consciousness, functionally, transcends the level of an individual, organization and community and has its main focus in societal learning and consciousness raising. Indeed, it acts as a veritable catalyst for the evolution of such rounded development, and thereby taps strongly into the cultural and spiritual sources of a particular society, serving to recognize and release its GENE-IUS.

In that process it renews the cultural and spiritual grounds of a such a community, organization and society and contributes to the "*regeneration of meaning*" as the main theme of the "*eastern*" realm. A primary case for this, as we saw in the final chapter of our previous volume on *Awakening*

Table 8.3 Developmental academy/awakening consciousness

Developmental academy: awakening integral consciousness Regenerates meaning via culture and spirituality Contributes to balanced and peaceful co-evolution

- *Focus*: catalyst for societal learning and consciousness raising / renews the cultural and spiritual sources of organization, community, society.
- *Required qualities of development catalyst*:

  ○ listening (picking up the implicit, behind the explicit messages);
  ○ reflective, intuitive and pattern-seeking mind;
  ○ will and ability to grow in consciousness;
  ○ ability to enter unknown, unfamiliar spaces;
  ○ able to engage with cultural/spiritual dynamics of a particular place;
  ○ able to question and to let go of one's own convictions and beliefs;
  ○ openness for surprising insights, and emerging patterns of culture;
  ○ ability to co-evolve with others, and to be a catalyst for the evolution of others.

- *Suggested symbol*: spiral of conscious co-evolution – represents regeneration and renewal of the culture and consciousness of a society.

integral consciousness, was that of Sarvodaya in Sri Lanka, albeit that there is not yet a uni-versity there to embody it. Over the past fifty years, as we saw, Sarvodaya engaged in *"the awakening of all"* (the translation of Sarvodaya), which comprised individual and community, national and world development.

While it has not yet set up tangible academy structures and systems, a "developmental academy", so to speak, is embedded in about 15,000 villages within Sri Lanka, in their political and economic processes. Addressing imbalances therein, Sarvodaya fosters a more *"balanced and peaceful co-evolution"* within Sri Lanka, the core *"eastern"* value, in between the diverse Sinhalese and Tamil groupings of society. In Table 8.4 we provide an overview of such a Developmental Academy structure and the Awakening of consciousness as a core function. We now turn to the reframed, innovation driven, institutionalized Research Academy.

Reframed Research Academy: institutionalized social research

Combining natural and social sciences, and the humanities

The integrally reframed Research Academy represents the culmination of the *"northern"* realm of knowledge. It is focused on scholarship, research and institutionalized knowledge creation aiming – simultaneously – for social and technological innovation. Natural sciences neither dominate, nor are they subordinated to, the social sciences, and the humanities are restored to their rightful place alongside both. Knowledge acquisition, moreover, is not regarded as static, but as continuously and dynamically unfolding. Research is seen as an "*art form*" fostering the originality of the researcher (and hence his/her potential to innovate). We now turn specifically to the notion of a "Mode 2" university, which serves to fundamentally reframe knowledge production, for us also incorporating pre-school, primary and secondary schools, and with which, alongside Da Vinci Institute in South Africa, Trans4m is closely associated.

Towards a Mode 2 Academy

Mode 1 versus Mode 2

Michael Gibbons (see Gibbons *et al.*, 1994), was Director of the Science Policy Research Unit at the University of Sussex, and Helga Nowotny (see Nowotny *et al.*, 2001) was Professor of Sociology at the Institute for Theory and Social Studies of Science at the University of Vienna, in the 1990s. Both were leading lights behind the idea of a "Mode 2" university, our partner institution Da Vinci Institute in South Africa, co-founded by Nelson Mandela in the new South Africa, being purportedly one such Mode 2 institution.

Table 8.4 Reframed Northern Research Academy

Reframed Research Academy Reframes knowledge via science, systems and technology Contributes to open and transparent knowledge creation

- *Focus*: on scholarship, research and knowledge creation aiming – simultaneously – for social and technological innovation.
- *Required qualities of integral researcher-and-innovator:*
  - conceptual and analytical strength;
  - ability to share knowledge in a team;
  - able to translate cultural images into concepts and theories;
  - able to deal with complexity;
  - intellectual explorer, adventurer of the mind;
  - ability to articulate and communicate new thoughts;
  - able to function within an institutionalized environment.
- *Suggested symbol*: grid of knowledge – represents intelligent, structure-seeking and organizing processes of knowledge creation.

Mode 2 knowledge production, for them, is different from Mode 1 in nearly every respect. The new mode operates in a context of application whereby problems are not set within a disciplinary framework. It is a trans-disciplinary rather than a mono- or even multidisciplinary entity. It is carried out in non-hierarchical, heterogeneously organized forms that are essentially transient. Mode 2 involves the close interaction of many actors throughout the process of knowledge production and this means that knowledge production is becoming more socially accountable. One consequence of this is that Mode 2 makes use of a wider range of criteria in judging quality control.

Overall, the process of knowledge production is becoming more reflexive and affects at the deepest levels what shall count as "good science". For many, Mode 1 is identical with what is meant by science. In Mode 1 as such, problems are set and solved in a context governed by the largely academic interests of a specific community. By contrast Mode 2 knowledge is carried out in the context of application. Mode 1 is disciplinary while Mode 2 is trans-disciplinary. Mode 1 is characterized by homogeneity while Mode 2 is heterogeneous. Organizationally, Mode 1 is hierarchical and tends to preserve its form, while Mode 2 is heterarchical and transient. Mode 2 is contextual and reflexive. All of this applies, for us then, as much to pre-, primary and secondary, as it does to tertiary research and education.

Rethinking science and society

The argument of Nowotny's *Rethinking Science: Knowledge and the Public in the Age of Uncertainty*, together with her colleagues (Nowotny *et al.*, 2001), is organized around the description of four interrelated processes. *First*, it is contended that the emergence of more open systems of knowledge production – Mode 2 science – and the growth of complexity and uncertainty in society – Mode 2 society – are phenomena linked in a co-evolutionary process. The implication is that *not only does science speak to society, but society speaks to science.*

Second, the process of *reverse communication is transforming science*, and this, in its simplest terms, *is what is meant by contextualization.* Moreover, and *third*, the process of contextualization moves science beyond merely reliable knowledge to *socially robust knowledge.* Neither state nor market, neither exclusively public or private, the *agora* is the space in which scientific and societal problems are framed and defined, and where what will be accepted as a "solution" is negotiated. *Fourth*, the range of perspectives found in the *agora*, together with the ability of their proponents to articulate their wishes and concerns as well as to mobilize resources for research activities, *implies a more complex role for scientific and technical expertise in the production of socially robust knowledge.* The novel factor is that the role of scientific and technical expertise is changing as it becomes more socially distributed. Openness to a great variety of knowledge traditions is a way of constantly reactivating the creativity of the core. These riches allow us to constantly reconfigure knowledge.

We now turn, fourth, to what we have termed the "academy of life", and the transformative approach to education therein.

The Academy of Life: Embodying integral development

A laboratory for creative experimentation

We turn, then, to the Academy of Life, institutionally, and to the Embodiment of integral development, functionally. The Academy of Life embodies the *"western"* realm of action, and is very much encouraged within our transformative educational programs, at Trans4m, as well as within those of the Ahliyyah School for Girls in Jordan and the Otona Zupancica Slovenska Bistrica Kindergarten in Slovenia. It can be described, as such, as a laboratory for creative experimentation, and as an educationally transformative, conducive space in which new individual, organizational and societal practices can be conceived of, tested and implemented. It represents new ways of learning and mirrors the growing desire for developmental–educational spaces that deal, hands on, via action learning and action research with the burning issues societies are facing.

Such Academies of Life are, then,

- embedded in the middle of *"real life"* (such as, for example, within an enterprise or a movement);
- linked to a sincere and systematic attempt to study and understand what life is about, how it works, what we can learn from nature, and how we live in nature – as a part of it – without harming it;
- enablers of *"whole life experiences"* – equally valuing inner and outer experiences, seeing the human being and human systems holistically;
- thriving, like nature, on interconnectedness, co-creation and co-evolution, with the Academy seeing itself as part of a living network of learning and action;
- like nature, spaces for experimentation and evolution – the Academy is a social laboratory, active as a developmental force, individually and collectively, in society.

Much of our own PHD (Process of Holistic Development) embodied in our PhD, undergraduate and organizational development programs, as well as the pre-school and school programs referred to earlier in the chapter, conforms to the above, but is not yet embodied within a whole new academy of life.

Recent proliferation of "universities of life"

Such a university in fact, and for example, may be the so-called Gaia University or the Giordano Bruno GlobalShift University, both initiated in central Europe, or indeed Ken Wilber's Ubiquity University in the United States. Such Universities of Life are therefore richly variegated in nature and scope. However, they are likely to primarily address the still relatively small "*species*" of the "*global citizen*" – inspired individuals with a global perspective who look for opportunities to learn and apply new skills for societal betterment. They therefore need to be complemented by "*southern*" Community Academies and "*eastern*" Developmental Academies as well as renewed "*northern*" Research Academies. At the same time, such "alternative" schools as the Steiner Waldorf Schools, as per Francis Edmund's *From Thinking to Living* (1990), and the Montessori Schools are variations on such an "academy of life" theme. Finally, as we saw in Chapter 1, "Constituting the South" (see Chancellor Williams above), the "age sets" referred to are very much in tune with such a life-laden approach.

Table 8.5 Academy of Life/Embodying integral development

University of Life
Capacity building
Contributes to development as a whole

- *Focus*: creative experimentation / conducive space in which new practices can be conceived of, tested and implemented.
- *Required qualities of learning facilitator*:

  o ability to team up with others;
  o ability to translate knowledge into capacities;
  o strong project management skills;
  o stamina and willingness to face and overcome obstacles on the way;
  o strong communication skills;
  o able to see one's own work as a contribution to a larger project.

- *Suggested symbol*: arrow of integrated action – represents focus, goal-oriented, co-creative realization of a new development impulse through actively building new infrastructure and institutions.

Conclusion

Integral academy in theory

In the final analysis, for all of the Academy types, the following applies:

- each can serve to complement, if not altogether reform the existing educational system of a society, at all levels;
- each is primarily an authentic articulation of one particular reality or worldview, applied to successive rounds;
- each thereby carries to some degree the other realities and realms within itself (e.g. Sarvodaya with its strong developmental orientation derived out of its cultural–spiritual perspective, also strongly focused on community needs).

In effect, moreover, each element – community academy, developmental, research and living academy – embodies our respective *CARE* functionalities, as well as providing an intimation of what such CARE structures may be like.

Integral academy in practice

In theory, then, the integral academy might be the appropriate way to institutionally go, *CARE* wise, most specifically here in relation to innovation driven, *institutionalized* research. In practice, however, at a university if not also secondary school level, as we have realized through our close association with both Heliopolis University for Sustainable Development (see Chapter 2) in Egypt (Mode 1) and Da Vinci Institute, our Trans4m partner in South Africa (Mode 2), the idealized integral design very quickly gets modified by the conventional university reality, both through standardized accreditation processes and through conventional academic patterns of thought and behaviour. Moreover, and most especially in the "global south" where resources are all too often scarce, research gets crowded out by courses. In fact, and altogether, the very notion of a *university*, or a *high school* as such, less so at primary and pre-school level, inhibits the CAREing designs and expectations we might have.

At Heliopolis University for Sustainable Development, in fact, students and faculty are simultaneously exposed to a humanistic core program, focusing on the inner development of the individual self in the context of group and community, and to specialist programs – on sustainable approaches to Business & Economics, Pharmacy, and Engineering. Learners and researchers, individually and collectively, are supposed to make a tangible outer contribution in their particular field, thereby engaging in the sustainable development of Egypt as a whole. This is achieved through its enriched educational curricula as well as learning and research processes, evolved out of our Trans4m integral approach, which can be aligned with CARE:

- *context: engaging with relevant context (Community activation);*
- *consciousness: raising of human consciousness (Awakening consciousness);*
- *content: assimilating inspiring content (innovation driven Research);*
- *contribution: making a significant contribution (Embody development).*

The university as a whole, however, in prospect if not altogether in reality – given the bureaucratic norms of a conventional Egyptian (if not worldwide) university structure and curriculum – is intended to be fully embedded in society, dealing concretely with its most burning socio-economic issues and innovating viable sustainable futures. The conservative Egyptian education authorities inevitably though, not to mention also some of the faculty – eager to follow established western standards rather than developing their own – have only partially then bought into Heliopolis University's new approach to curriculum content (focus on sustainable development) and educational design (the above 4 C's). However, notwithstanding the above, as the university opened its doors in autumn 2012, it did so as one of world's first universities with an exclusive thematic focus on sustainable development.

It is for that very reason, ultimately, while building on such CARE-ing constituents, processually and functionally, we turn to what we have termed an *Institutional Genealogy*, structurally and formally, for our *reasoned realization*, which is no longer inhibited by conventional university or school structures and processes. To that extent, simultaneously and interactively, *while a community academy serves to institutionalize community activation, a developmental academy serves to awaken integral consciousness applied to enterprise, economy and development, a research academy underlies innovation driven, institutionalized research, an academy of life is one where integral development is fully embodied,* and *each form of academy ultimately complements the other.*

We now turn to our institutional genealogy, thereby reinventing knowledge.

References

Edmunds, F. (1990) *From Thinking to Living: The Work of Rudolf Steiner.* Shaftesbury, Dorset: Element Books.

Gibbons, M., Limoges, C., Nowotny, H., Schwartzman, S., Scott, P. and Trow, M. (1994) *The New Production of Knowledge: The Dynamics of Science and Research in Contemporary Societies.* London: Sage.

Nowotny, H., Scott, P. and Gibbons, M. (2001) *Re-Thinking Science: Knowledge and the Public in the Age of Uncertainty.* Cambridge: Polity.

Schieffer, A. and Lessem, R. (2014) *Integral Development: Realising the Transformative Potential of Individuals, Organizations, Societies.* Abingdon: Routledge.

9 Reinventing knowledge
Integral dynamics

Summary of chapter:

1 we conceive of an integrated Genealogy rather than a standardized University;
2 research is aligned with community, sanctuary, academy, laboratory;
3 there is connection and renewal of oral, scriptural, textual and digital forms;
4 such interactive linkages lead to release of GENE-ius/recognizing GENEalogy.

Introduction: integral dynamics and the path of renewal

Integral academy to inter-institutional genealogy

In Chapter 7 we called for a newly *integral, social research* paradigm, starting out with a *relational* focus on a particular society, community or organization, rather than following, altogether, universalist research and innovation principles. Thereafter, in Chapter 8, we envisioned, on the path of renewal, what an *integral academy*, including school and university, might look like. We now, as Chapter 9, along the way to emancipatory navigation, with a view to innovation driven, institutionalized research, transform the university into a newly structured as well as newly functioning *Inter-Institutional Genealogy*, thereby reinventing knowledge. Such a *reasoned realization*, in form as well as function, of CARE, in fact forms the key chapter in this particular volume.

The impetus to inter-institutional *Genealogy*, then, building upon Pax Africana, based in Nigeria (see Chapter 4), is our integral recognition that there is a need for a totally new CARE-ing entity, in fact the kind of entity that could take Integral Green Zimbabwe, and Slovenia (see previous chapters, 5 and 6) sustainably on, in both functionally dynamical and structurally stabilizing terms. Indeed, from our longstanding experience, with universities in the west (USA and UK) and north (Continental Europe), south (South Africa, Zimbabwe, Nigeria, Brazil and Argentina) and east (China, Japan, India), over the past four decades, including such evolved examples as Heliopolis University and Da Vinci Institute (see previous chapter), we have found the following: their very university-based stabilizing structures, including globalized accreditation procedures, graduation rituals, individual course and student orientations, serve to inhibit our overall, integral orientation, not to mention the fact that they by-pass pre-primary, primary and secondary education. As a result, all too often, and as we have seen in South Africa and Nigeria for example, students disrupt this structure by way of dysfunctional, political dynamics.

We need to start afresh, but inclusively rather than exclusively, by duly reinventing knowledge, functionally and structurally, acknowledging that in specific instances schools may offer more fertile grounds than universities.

Reinventing knowledge: orientation to genealogy

To help us along that newly global way we have drawn on two significant sources across the Atlantic: the French post-modern philosopher Michel Foucault (Prado, 2000), through specifically his notion of *Genealogy*, and the University of Oregon-based cultural historians McNeely and Wolverton, in their *Re-inventing Knowledge* (2008). We also refer to our own previous work *Integral Dynamics: Cultural Dynamics, Political Economy and the Future of the University* (Lessem *et al.*, 2013).

We thereby take a hard look at the sources and development of the key educational notions and ideas we take to be central to, and definitive of, what concerns us. That means not "totalizing" knowledge, functionally, as per the modern university, with its standardized, MBA-like (Harvard University) or

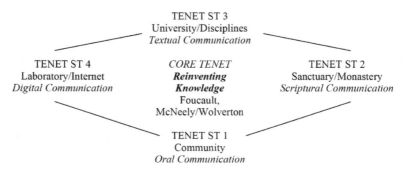

Figure 9.1 Institutional research realization: navigation tenets.

PPE-like (Oxford University) offerings, but rather effecting history across our *integral realms*, through natural, cultural, scientific and economic *Genealogy*. We need then, following Foucault, a particular historical awareness of our present circumstance. *That awareness problematizes current truths by tracing their descent and emergence, and by uncovering alternatives, each one in its particular individual, institutional and societal context.* We start, functionally and genealogically, in philosophical terms, with Foucault.

Thereafter we turn, structurally, to our own institutional GENE-alogy, duly informed by the American cultural historians McNeely and Wolverton, and their historical reinvention of knowledge structures.

Foucault on genealogy

Genealogical inversion of the universal over the particular

The French post-modernist philosopher and social activist Michel Foucault in fact, in the period between the 1950s and the 1980s, dedi-cated himself to functionally *counter-acting the prevailing "modern" rationality, or conventional "scientific" wisdom, presented by "north-western" universities and academics as dominant, and endowed with the status of one-and-only reason.* He wanted to demonstrate that such ration-ality, as indeed conveyed by academe then and now, most specifically in the human sciences, whether at school or at university, is only one philosophical approach among others, indeed for us only one of three or four fundamental alternatives, each with different underlying worldviews (realities) and respective integral trajectories (rhythms).

In fact *Nietzsche's inversion of the particular over the universal was a philosophical revolution*, for Foucault's Guatemalan-born, *genealogi-cal* interpreter C.G. Prado (now Emeritus Professor in the Department of Philosophy at Queen's University, Ontario, Canada), which *was as momen-tous as Kant's "Copernican" inversion of the subjective over the objective.* Foucault then emulates Nietzsche with three inversions of his own. He inverts the interpretive significance of the marginal (social majority – our "south" and "east") over the ostensibly central (economic elite – our "north-west"); he inverts the socially constructed over the supposedly natu-ral (e.g. "natural" laws of the market versus now *socially* constructed); and he inverts the originative and foundational importance of (our grounding) his emergent, and the thereby indeterminate, over the allegedly inevitable and determinate (our navigation and effect).

At a very abstract level, these inversions constitute the core of what is novel about Foucault's thought. Nietzsche and Foucault show, then, that, *rather than uniformity, what is found at the historical beginning of things is disparity*, for us between "north" and "south", "east" and "west", communally so to speak, as well as our integral realms. Thereby, additionally and dynamically, the release of GENE-ius requires us to interweave, and thereby co-evolve, one with the other, with the marginalized "south" gaining pride of at least starting place.

From genealogy to GENEalogy

While Foucault specifically, however, and post-modernists generally, champion "many truths" over such a single one, and thereby have a more emancipatory view of the world than their more universalist, modern counterparts, they fail to particularize the identity of specific groups of people. While we at Trans4m run the risk of over-GENE-ralization through our "integral realities", and perhaps overplay the cultural, and underplay the political, we do pay special attention to *releasing the genius of each nature and community, culture and spirituality, through a science and technology, economy, and overall polity, that fits each one.* In other words, we start out by recognizing, and drawing upon, the Grounding – *relational, renewal wise or reasoned realization* – of a society. The same disparities, as we shall see, underlie the particular communities on which our institutional genealogies are based.

This befits our GENE (Lessem *et al.*, 2013; see "Awakening integral consciousness", Chapter 5). After G̲rounding, dynamically speaking, come E̲mergence, N̲avigation and E̲ffect, if you like GENEalogy of a different kind. Moreover, Foucault, for all his philosophical genius, never attempted to create the kind of institution that would reflect his genealogical orientation. The question is, what kind of new genealogical agency, or indeed institutional genealogy, as different from a standardized, centralized university, can put this GENE-alogy into effect? We now turn to McNeely and Wolverton to take our story on, building also on the prior genealogical–institutional functioning we saw in Nigeria (Chapter 4).

Reinventing knowledge

Two American Oregon University-based historians of knowledge, husband-and-wife partnership Ian McNeely and Lisa Wolverton, wrote a seminal book in the first decade of the new millennium titled *Reinventing Knowledge: From Alexandria to the Internet* (2008). In it they introduce six institutions that, for them, have served to build up the knowledge that we all have today.

Three of these are the *monastery* (which we now term a "sanctuary" to avoid any particular religious and also purely human, devoid of natural, connotations); the *university*; and a *laboratory*. These, then, are key constituents

Table 9.1 Integral genealogy

Innovation driven institutionalized research: path of reason Reinventing knowledge Contributes to a university of the future
• *Communal attributes*: <u>Grounding</u> – Constituting Africa, Sekem Commonwealth, European Compass; <u>Emergence</u> – social research paradigm, social ecology, integral development; <u>Navigation</u> – communitalism, integral university, *reinventing knowledge*; <u>Effect</u> – social economy, knowledge creation, solidarity economy. • *Integrator role*: researcher and innovator, e.g. ***Foucault, McNeely, Wolverton***. • *Research function*: scholarship, research and knowledge creation on ***integral dynamics and the future of the academy***. • *Navigating knowledge creation*: such research is embodied in the ***community, sanctuary, academy and laboratory***; connecting ***oral, scriptural, textual and digital***; such interactive linkages lead to states the ***release of GENE-ius*** – problems tackled ***genealogically, going to the roots***.

of our Institutional *Genealogy*, as we shall see, to which we add a fourth genealogical agency, that is, natural and social *Community* of both physical and human species, inclusive of all living matter. The other three entities for McNeely and Wolverton, that is the Library, the so-called "Republic of Letters", and the Disciplines, for us, constitute intermediate, transitional categories. Genealogy, from an institutional perspective overall, is then, for us, the ultimately integral dynamic, agential category, incorporating *Community, Sanctuary, Academy and Laboratory* altogether. These moreover, and in turn, as we shall see, build further upon, while ultimately serving to transform, the integral academy that has come before. We turn first to nature and community.

Grounding and origination in oral *community*: healing power to Socratic method

The healing power of nature

Nature in fact, for Father Anselm Adodo of Paxherbals in Nigeria, as we saw in Chapter 4, is the foundation of life, and source of healing, of both individual and community. Without nature, concepts of community, purpose and healing would be meaningless. In other words, *every tree, plant, hill, mountain, rock, speaks for itself as it were, and as such vibrates as a subtle energy that has healing power whether we know it or not.*

For California-based Burkina Faso-born writer and elder Malidoma Patrice Somé, in his book *The Healing Wisdom of Africa* (1999), the community exists, at least in part, *to safeguard the purpose of each person within it and to awaken the memory of that purpose by recognizing the unique gifts each brings to the world.*

Revisiting the orally based Socratic method

Socrates, to whom we were introduced in Chapter 3, as an elder and oral philosopher in ancient Greece, for McNeely and Wolverton – like such an elder as Somé in Africa – hearkened back to the living, verbal bonds among men, and to the oral pedagogy founded on the productive interchange between masters and students. In his case this took place through the "Socratic method" of robust question and answer, our source of communal origination. This also reflected *Socrates' belief that the interchange of speech leads to truth. The written word, by contrast, is untrustworthy and corrupting because it is detached from the actions, honour and character of whoever uttered it.*

Building on the Communitalism

Finally, and institutionally as intimated in Chapter 8 above on the would-be *integral Academy*, the *Community*, as a genealogical entity, builds upon the *Communitalism* and indeed *Community activation*, whereby:

- *as a contextualized platform for communal learning and development, communities are enabled to reclaim their full problem-solving potential;*
- *communal stewards deeply immerse themselves in a particular natural and communal context, able to relate to other human beings and to nature;*
- *the stewards embody the web of life representing interdependency, the circle of physical and human nature reflecting the original oneness of all creation.*

We now turn from community to sanctuary.

Emerging foundation: scriptural monastery–sanctuary

Spiritual and psychological confessions

If a particular indigenous community, as per Paxherbals (see Chapter 4), serves to orally ground research and education, learning and knowledge creation, what we term a *sanctuary* (McNeely's monastery as per the Benedictine Monastery to which Father Anselm Adodo belongs), histori-cally takes knowledge scripturally on from there. We now turn, therefore, to the influence of the sacred: our genealogical foundation.

Thanks in no small part to Augustine's *Confessions*, for example in the fourth century AD, based in what is now Algeria, Christian scripture, according to McNeely, began to displace Roman rhetoric most specifi-cally *in the emergence of personal character and values.* Similar texts were developed by Hindu and Buddhist, Jewish and Muslim scholars (see for example the influence of the Islamic *madrassahs* in the ninth to thirteenth centuries) over time. *The emphasis* now for us, in all of this, *was not only on service to the community, naturally and socially, but also as such, on wholeness or on holiness*, anticipating awakening of integral consciousness, from one or other spiritual and/or religious source. In this way, we build on the foundations of a *developmental* "university", whereby:

- *individual and collective learning and consciousness raising serves to renew cultural and spiritual sources of organization, community, society;*
- *a development catalyst is able to engage with cultural/spiritual dynam-ics of a particular entity/place, able to co-evolve with individual/ institutional others;*
- *a spiral of conscious co-evolution represents the regeneration and renewal of the spirit, culture and consciousness of a person/enterprise/ place.*

Unfortunately somewhat dogmatic immersion in "religion", as opposed to the original Latin meaning of *re-ligere*, literally for us, as for Adodo as we have seen, as a re-visiting and renewal of your origins, all too often conceals this e-ducative and e-mergent aspect of such culture and spirituality. Indeed in our acculturating terms, such re-ligion draws you back into your own inner depths, and outwardly across in trans-cultural relation to the other, by way of inter-faith dialogue. The Islamic Renaissance was indeed a good historical case in point.

Islamic cultural and spiritual renaissance

From the ninth to the thirteen centuries, according to McNeely and Wolverton, there was an Islamic Renaissance, in which the *madrassahs* – starting out in Morocco in the ninth century – played a leading part in Muslim prayer, contemplation and learning, prior to the formation of the universities in the Middle East and Europe. Indeed Baghdad had fol-lowed in the footsteps of the great Alexandrian library in Egypt. Its *House of Wisdom, founded around 800 BC, gathered a multicultural scholarly community to translate all known exemplars of "foreign wisdom" into Arabic.* In fact the Islamic mosque today, at least in some notable cases, remains a place of learning, as well as prayer.

To that extent the link between the scriptural (*religare* – renewal) and the literal (*sapiens* – knowledge) was forged. The Judeo-Christian and Islamic monotheism, of course, was preceded by Hindu polytheism.

Indian Ashram: source of spiritual enlightenment

Today many an Indian *ashram*, moreover, is a place of not only prayer, but also meditation, yoga and other such pursuits geared towards spiritual enlightenment, to which many a "western seeker" is attracted. While generally these are Hindu based, there are also Buddhist retreats, in for example Korea and Japan, where such spiritual contemplation is, and has been, undertaken, now as well as in prior centuries. Many westerners now join in such practices, both at home and abroad. However, such so-called "esoteric" pursuits are conventionally divorced from mainstream education and research, in the university, and all too often individualized rather than institutionalized.

We now turn, guided by McNeely and Wolverton, to the pursuit of scientific knowledge per se, as well as the humanities, via the original "universitas", the subsequently so-called "republic of letters", and ultimately the research university, and its constituent "disciplines". Altogether then *genealogically, community, sanctuary and university constitute a formidable, developmental force, to be followed by the laboratory, if purposefully combined in a particular context.* How, then, did the original universities actually get started?

Navigating emancipation via print: academy, science and technology

The communal universitas

Starting with the earliest forms of European university (universities in China, India and the Middle East having been established centuries before), in the twelfth and thirteenth centuries in Bologna and Paris, these were not deliberately founded; they simply *coalesced spontaneously around networks of students and teachers, as nodes at the thickest in these networks.* "Universitas", for McNeely and Wolverton, as such, was a concept in ancient Roman law referring to a sworn society of individuals, that is, to a group of people, not a physical space. In fact the early universities retained some of the communal attributes of pre-modern oral cultures, and of ancient times. They also had, from the outset, strongly theological, scriptural overtones.

Initial schools or faculties: theology, medicine, law, liberal arts

By 1200, McNeely and Wolverton went on to say, Paris had become known as the international centre for *theology*. Other scholarly pilgrimage sites developed academic schools or "faculties": *law* in Bologna, *medicine* in Salerno, and much later the *liberal* arts in Prague. The revival of Roman law, in fact, marked one of the great intellectual movements of the twelfth century. *Whereas Roman law was rational yet individualistic, German custom*, however fuzzily, *was much more imbued with community spirit. In their synthesis lie the origins of the universitas as legal concept and social reality.*

We now turn from the early academic schools, as separate entities, to the newly emerging scientific communities that served to link, as a means of emancipatory navigation, in our genealogical terms so to speak, one with the other. Here we have a scientific – rather than religious – vocation, source of scholarship, and communal learning, now internationally as well as nationally and locally oriented, coming for the first time together, as a "republic of letters".

Interregnum: republic of letters – international learning community

Inspired by humanistic discourse

The so-called "Republic of Letters", representing a kind of interregnum between orality and literacy, according to McNeely and Wolverton, can be defined as an international community of learning stitched together initially by handwritten letters in the mail, and later by printed books and journals. The term is ancient in origin: it hearkens back to the Roman orator Cicero. The Ciceronian ideal of a *respublica literaria* was revived imitatively when it re-entered European usage in the late fifteenth century. Shorn of its political connotations in its later incarnation, this ideal inspired new practices of humanistic discourse among men and women of letters. The republic of letters, then, newly founded its legitimacy in the production of new knowledge. Why did this happen at this particular place, and point in time, in the eighteenth century?

All its members were considered equal

The republic of letters, in fact, was constituted at the moment that politicized religion tore Europe apart. *In conditions of crisis, it emerged as an alternative, secular institution of learning, partly rivalling, partly complementing the old universities by knitting European learning newly together.* Such a "republic", moreover, recognized no distinctions of birth, social status, gender or academic degree. It rose above differences of language (Latin reigned supreme as the scholarly tongue), nationality or, especially, religion. It kept Protestant and Catholics in communication even when their faiths were at war. *All its members were considered equal. Entrance was purely informal, though there was a clear expectation that one would acquit oneself like a gentleman or gentlewoman.* Today, we might be calling for the equivalent "republic", across the whole of our troubled world, rather than just through Europe.

With traditional intellectual authorities in retreat, laypeople took unprecedented initiative in founding these new communities of learning. Such traditional authorities, moreover, straddled east and west, north and south, though, conventionally speaking today, the "north-western" academic "priesthood", so to speak, predominated, notwithstanding such a diverse heritage, which in fact underlay the creation of universities throughout the world.

Academic disciplines and the emergence of the Research Academy

Research University aimed to reshape the inner person

In fact *Europe's and indeed America's leading universities in modern times,* according to McNeely and Wolverton, *that is in the late eighteenth and early nineteenth centuries, counted among the last places most Enlightenment figures looked for to rejuvenate knowledge.* The same might apply, arguably for us, at least in the social sciences and humanities, if not also in the natural sciences, today! Oxford and Cambridge, for example, were better known for polishing the manners of young gentlemen than for sending them on to more serious pursuits. The story of how Germany led the world into the age of modern scholarship therefore counts among the most stunning reversals in the history of knowledge.

Founded initially in 1738, and as a predecessor to such a research university, *the seminar approach to pedagogy, launched at the University of Göttingen in Germany, aimed to reshape the inner person, not to fashion cookie-cutter gentlemen* by drilling them, as was hitherto customary in the prestigious universities, to ape Cicero or Pericles in their outward manners and speech. Instead they instilled in their students an internalized sense of what it meant to think like a Cicero. *The hierarchy of the medieval disputation, where masters often literally stood on platforms above their students, gave way to "circular disputation", where discussants sat around a table together as equals.* Beyond how Cicero spoke, beyond what Jesus said, beyond what Homer sang, for McNeely and Wolverton, students and their professors reflected on how cultures think, collectively and creatively, through the study of philology. *Scholarship had finally replaced scripture as the ultimate source of human knowledge.*

From scholarship to the promotion of ideas: the case of Karl Marx

At the same time, academic entrepreneurs with a taste for risk could throw in their lot with profit-driven, or indeed socially motivated, publishing ventures. This was the career path chosen, ironically enough, by Karl Marx for example. He began as a typical academic, writing a dissertation on Greek natural philosophy at the University of Berlin. But his politics forced him out of Berlin's conservative establishment and he then spent several years in Paris, Brussels and the Rhineland gaining notoriety or fame, depending on your viewpoint, as editor and contributor to a series of radical newspapers. Conflict with censors and stockholders kept his writings from making money, but Marx ultimately found an investor, once he had immigrated to Britain, in Friedrich Engels, the son of a wealthy industrialist, who also became his intellectual collaborator.

The disciplines reached out to the educated masses

At the same time, in bringing the panoply of knowledge to publics eager for education, whether at school or university level, the disciplines thus fulfilled what had been the dream of the Enlightenment all along – to reach the masses. Lasting success, though, in the natural sciences required, in addition to the seminar, the institution of the laboratory, the ultimate step in McNeely and Wolverton's journey from community to our sanctuary, to university on to laboratory, and for us altogether on to genealogy. Altogether, then, in all-round genealogical terms these become vehicles for the promotion of learning and development, research and innovation: individually, organizationally, societally.

Specifically for our purposes, then, the *research* academy is indeed the only part of the fourfold genealogy that resonates with what we conventionally recognize as a school or a university, within which:

- *scholarship, research and knowledge creation aim – in conjunction with the other genealogical entities – for social innovation;*
- *the social researcher-and-innovator as such has conceptual and analytical ability, is able to share knowledge in a group and is able to deal with complexity;*
- *the resulting grid of knowledge represents intelligent, structure-seeking and organizing processes of knowledge creation across recognized disciplines.*

We finally turn to the laboratory.

The laboratory effect: NASA, counterculture, worldwide web

The world as laboratory

Starting out in the natural sciences, in the nineteenth century, for McNeely and Wolverton, *laboratory scientists, after learning to control nature within the four walls of their experimental domains, capitalized on their methods to change the way people lived in homes, neighbourhoods, even whole countries.*

Louis Pasteur, for example, as a prominent exemplar in France (1822–1895), began his research life as a chemist. Microbes became his research speciality. Today the simple technique of pasteurization, now so-called flash-heating of milk to kill bacteria and delay their return at cooler temperatures, applies Pasteurian microbiology to every household refrigerator. *In reshaping our domestic environment, Pasteur's science literally made the world into a laboratory.* Starting in 1910, Pasteur Institutes began to be established throughout France's overseas colonies (in Tunis, Tangiers, Casablanca, Saigon and Dakar) and beyond (in Sao Paulo, Shanghai, Teheran and Bangkok). *These laboratories made imperial France's medical science a key component of its "civilizing" mission abroad.*

Why, then, for McNeely, did Pasteur prevail in such a prolific way? *His approach*, in effect, *meshed with networks of social, economic, and political power*: the farm interests, the government statisticians, the overseas colonists. To these powerful interests he added that of the laboratory scientist. *Pasteurian science proved once and for all the social utility of the laboratory, the very real ways in which it could improve human life*, as would be the case a century later for the exploration of outer space, ultimately leading to the late President Kennedy's one giant step forward for mankind.

NASA Space Agency: a giant step forward for mankind

In 1969, at the height of the cold war, NASA director James Webb published *Space Age Management*, heralding the application of social-scientific techniques to the one space still unconquered by the laboratory: the cosmos itself. In five years *the NASA workforce had grown to 420,000 people, dispersed in scores of universities, laboratories, government agencies and industrial contractors. The craftsman's workshop had given way to adaptive problem solving*, diverse specialists linked together by coordinating processes in organic flux. Lamentably, for us, nothing like this exists in the social sciences.

Yet, for McNeely and Wolverton, the institutional building blocks of big science were well in place by the beginning of the twenty-first century. As such, these were simply *the twin guises of the laboratory, physical (to a greater extent) and social (to a lesser extent)*, fused together. Yet, for all the dazzling technologies that have emerged over the course of the last century, there has been little further institutional innovation, beyond the laboratory, to purposefully address the kinds of problems we face today in any fundamental way.

The advent of the internet and the World Wide Web in the 1990s

A core feature of today's knowledge society is the networked computer, an information appliance born in the laboratory and democratized by both public and private enterprise. Born in a climate overshadowed by war and the use of science for weapons development, computers and computer networks spread in short order to research universities, corporate installations, and ultimately the wider consumer market. Indeed for the originator of the World Wide Web, Berners Lee,

> The Web is more of a social creation than a technical one. I designed it for a social effect – to help people work together – and not as a technical toy. The ultimate goal of the Web, for me, is to support and improve our web-like existence in the world . . . . *While business, government and other such bodies often wish to "control" the web, to further each of their interests, they are the background to the Web, as far as I am concerned, not the foreground . . . the Web's universality leads to a thriving richness and diversity.* (Berners Lee, 1999)

The scientific laboratory in which Berners Lee was based, while evolving the World Wide Web, was CERN in Geneva, much more renowned now for its breakthroughs in contemporary physics than in the social or even systems sciences: this brings us back to the argument advanced in the last chapter, whereby technological invariably trumps social, innovation. To the extent that such a laboratory fosters social innovation, it becomes:

- *a focal point for creative experimentation / a conducive space in which new social and economic practices can be conceived of, tested and implemented;*
- *a space where a learning facilitator as such is able to team up with others, to translate knowledge into capacities, having strong project management skills;*
- *focused, goal oriented, co-creative, resulting in the active build-up of new infrastructure and institutions.*

Conclusion: community, sanctuary, academy, laboratory

The question then is, by way of conclusion, what is the real difference between the integral academy and the newly structurally constituted *institutional genealogy*, given that Community activation (community academy–*community*–grounding), Awakening of integral consciousness (developmental academy–*sanctuary*–emergence), innovation driven Research (research academy–*academy*–navigation) and the Embodiment of integral development (academy of life–*laboratory*–effect) are incorporated within both? The key difference is that in the latter case the academy, whether pre-school, school or university, is only a structural part (arguably 25 per cent) of an integral whole, and is as such a specifically *research* academy, whereby *education* becomes part of the *laboratory*.

Inevitably we find, *when alluding to even an integral "university", if not also a "school" in that respect, one's mind inevitably turns to individual students, courses and accreditation, all too often disconnected from the vital needs, capacities and indeed history of a particular community.* Genealogically, then, such individual learning, for us, is recast in laboratory guise, thereby also duly aligned with organizational learning. Moreover, community building (community), consciousness raising (sanctuary) and knowledge creation (research academy) are equally par for the functional and structural genealogical course. At the same time and of equal importance, bureaucratic accreditation processes then only apply to a small, albeit significant part, of a whole, and even as such are recast in overall, genealogical terms. Thereby, for example on our Trans4m/Da Vinci PhD/PHD program, we introduce both individual and also collective accreditation, and the personal as well as communal rituals to go with each.

Overall, then, in the institutional genealogical case, *innovation driven institutional research is aligned with community, sanctuary, academy and laboratory, connecting and renewing oral, scriptural, textual and digital forms; such interactive linkages lead to states that release GENE-ius and recognize GENEalogy; problems are thereby tackled genealogically, going back to the roots, incorporating as such the universal future of the particular past.* This lies at the heart of our functional, dynamic *CARE* and structural, stabilizing CARE.

We now turn from this Integral Genealogy, modelled on Foucault, McNeely and Wolverton, by way of navigation, to the integral effect of institutional research, starting with the relational, social and economic path. As such, our *Institutional Genealogy* holds a pivotal, emancipatory position between grounding and emergence, which come genetically before, and ultimate effect, thereafter.

References

Berners Lee, T. (1999) *Weaving the Web.* San Francisco, CA: Harper & Row.
Lessem, R. Schieffer, A. and Rima, S.D. (2013) *Integral Dynamics: Cultural Dynamics, Political Economy and the Future of the University.* Abingdon: Routledge.
McNeely, I., and Wolverton, L. (2008) *Reinventing Knowledge: From Alexandria to the Internet.* New York: Norton.
Prado, C.G. (2000) *Starting with Foucault: An Introduction to Genealogy,* 2nd edition. Boulder, CO: Westview Press.
Somé, M. (1999) *The Healing Wisdom of Africa.* New York: Jeremy Tarcher.

Part IV

Effect of institutionalized research

10 Social economy

Social economics to cooperative enterprise

Summary of chapter:

1 innovation driven institutionalized research is grounded in social economics and the socialization of knowledge;
2 this emerges through personalism, corporativism and participation;
3 it is navigated through the collaboration of three main agents – universities, technology centres and companies;
4 altogether, these effect social transformation;
5 this culminates in a <u>cooperatively based social economy</u>.

Introduction: Mondragon – the relational path of navigation

Cooperative genealogy

In this next *relational* chapter on the transformative *effect* of innovation driven institutionalized research, also with a view to an effective inter-institutional ecology, at now both micro and macro levels, we turn to the renowned case of the Mondragon Cooperatives in the Spanish Basque country. Therein, social economics of old, reaching back to such pioneering thinkers as Sismondi in Switzerland, Ruskin and Hobson in Britain, and Gandhi in India, culminates in cooperative enterprise, which is the result of further, pioneering, subsequently institutionalized, social research by the founder of Mondragon. Specifically, then, the Mondragon Cooperatives, today the world's largest set of worker-owned industrial cooperatives, was founded midway through the last century by Father Arizmendiarrietta in the Spanish Basque country, as the result of innovation based, ultimately institutionally based, research, in turbulent times in the 1940s.

In genealogical terms, the Mondragon Cooperatives themselves constitute the laboratory, Arizmendiarrietta's original philosophical and spiritual impulse constitutes a sanctuary, accompanying the cooperatives is a research university, and the Basque region is the formative community, albeit, by way of such social and economic enterprise effect, the laboratories/cooperatives loom large.

Introduction to the Mondragon model

Mondragon today has established research centres, banks and credit unions, a university, youth cooperatives, and small to large businesses. Founded in 1956 in the Basque town of Mondragon, the cooperatives now encompass 264 businesses and employ more than 100,000 worker–owners in more than forty countries. And they began their life on the social research and development initiative of Don Jose Maria Arizmendiarrietta (Arizmendi), a rural village priest with a transformative vision, and strongly emancipatory knowledge foundation, who believed in the values of worker collaboration and working hard to reach for, and realize, the common good, starting out from his Basque community.

In its specific mission, then, for Mondragon analysts, American anthropologists William and Kathleen Whyte, *Mondragon describes itself as a "business-based socio-economic initiative with deep roots in the Basque Country, created for and by people and inspired by the basic principles of our cooperative experience"* (Whyte and Whyte, 1991).

Mondragon moreover operates on the basis of ten basic principles. These principles are *open admission, democratic organization, sovereignty of labour, the subordinate nature of capital, participatory management, payment solidarity, inter-cooperation, social transformation, universality and education.* Now we turn to the origins and philosophical underpinnings of Mondragon.

TENETS LF 3
Personalism, Cooperativism, Participation

TENETS LF 4
Social
Transformation

CORE TENET LF
Social Economy

TENETS LF2
Inter-cooperation:
University,
Technology Centre,
Company

TENETS LF1
Sovereignty of Labour/Subordinated Capital

Figure 10.1 Mondragon effect: institutional R & D – relational.

Origins and philosophical foundation of Mondragon

Community, sanctuary and laboratory

The arrival of Arizmendiarrietta in February 1941, at Mondragon, a small town in the Basque country, in Spain, was "singularly unimpressive" (Whyte and Whyte, 1991). He never mastered the oratorical style of his priestly predecessors. But *he was shaping his own social gospel, in marked contrast to the traditional preoccupations of most of his fellow priests, who were concerned with individual salvation.* In his sermons and writings, *he stressed that work should not be seen as a punishment but as a means of self-realization. He spoke of the need for cooperation and collective solidarity.* He combined a social vision with an emphasis on education for technical knowledge and skills. He embodied, through initially following the Catholic social encyclicals, what we termed in the previous chapter the fruits of a progressive papal sanctuary.

Serving as a researcher and a teacher as well as a preacher, Don Jose Maria Arizmendiarrietta infused the institution-building process with the social vision that would subsequently guide the Mondragon movement.

Socializing knowledge within the Basque community

During interviews with the American authors of *Making Mondragon*, cited above, they described the way Arizmendi interpreted the beginnings of the movement:

> . . . *it is necessary to socialize knowledge in order to democratize power because in fact knowledge is power . . . . It therefore involved, in the early days, a process of mobilization, consciousness-raising and training, of theory and practice, of self-management and self-government, of young people. It was these youth who later would become protagonists of the cooperative experience . . . .* (Whyte and Whyte, 1991)

Moreover, Jose Maria Ormaechea, one of the five founders of Ulgor, the first of the cooperative steel foundries to be established in the 1950s, in recalling his early years with Arizmendi, wrote:

> *Don Jose Maria's fundamental gift was his capacity for personal dialogue. He treated us with affection but urged us every day to make a greater commitment to the labor movement and to the future economic and social transformation of society . . . necessary to change the sovereignty of capital to that of labor.* (Azurmendi, 1984)

For another of the founders, Alfonso Gorronogoitia, the drive towards personal mastery and competence did not submerge social and religious values:

> *What surprised other entrepreneurs was the poetic–philosophical tone that we adopted as industrial entrepreneurs. This humanistic inclination that surprised people we owe to Don Jose Maria, because we could never dissociate our entrepreneurial attitudes from a philosophy, a concept, an ideology, after the contact we had with him. We could not be pure technocrats, who knew perfectly the process of chemistry or physics or semi-conductors and nothing more.* (Azurmendi, 1984)

Adding elements of a research university

Don Jose Maria never developed his ideas systematically in a book, but he spoke and wrote constantly. Joxe Azurmendi in his 1984 book *El Hombre Cooperative: Pensamiento de Jose Maria Arizmendiarrieta* made an exhaustive analysis of his writings and placed them in the political and economic context of his times. Azurmendi describes the evolution of his thinking. In his first writings, in the early 1940s, the crisis of the times is seen as a crisis of faith, although seen in terms of a specific system of Christian–humanist values. By about 1945–50, Arizmendi was centring his attention on the social question. The nucleus of the crisis was no longer one of faith but that of property. After this epoch, distinctly religious themes seem to disappear from his writings.

Along with this evolution of ideas, Don Jose Maria shifted his attention from the family to the factory. In his first years in Mondragon he had been grappling with issues of housing and health, but now he focused ever more on the workplace. Among secular authors, meanwhile, Don Jose had closely researched the writings of the leftist Catholic French social philosophers Jacques Maritain (Maritain, 1996) and Emmanuel Mounier (Mounier, 1989). He was also influenced by the renowned Brazilian pedagogue Paulo Freire (Freire, 2000) and by the sayings of Mao Tse Tung.

Political ideology and religious faith

Arizmendi had several close friends and admirers among the clergy, but the Catholic Church did not provide institutional support for his work or for the Mondragon cooperative movement. He was, like his fellow Catholic and Benedictine monk Father Dr Anselm Adodo in Nigeria, as we saw (Chapter 4), highly critical of formal religion in general and of his church in particular:

In the name of religion, what barbarities have been committed. We must be on guard against any form of dogmatism . . . . Religion has been well marketed, but what good has it done? It has led us to feel the importance of the universal and the abstract. Theologians, sociologists, philosophers have operated from the top down, when the correct way to think is in the opposite direction. (Azurmendi, 1984)

At the same time he was allergic to all isms: 'Isms imprison and oppress us'. He wrote, though, as a researcher into cooperativism, that this is,

The third way distinct from egoist capitalism and from depersonalizing socialism. We want cooperatives, which constitute a new social potential and, thus, are built by those who are not impelled by a myopic and limited egotism or by a simple gregarious instinct. (Azurmendi, 1984)

On another occasion he wrote:

It is a monstrosity that a system of social organization is tolerated in which some can take advantage of the work of others for their exclusive personal profit . . . . The cooperativist distinguishes himself from the capitalist, simply in that the latter utilizes capital in order to make people serve him, while the former uses it to make more gratifying and uplifting the working life of the people. (Azurmendi, 1984)

Azurmendi (1984) warned against the complacency that often comes with success and stressed the need for constant re-evaluation of the cooperative experience:

Let us move ahead with criticisms and self-criticism more than with criticisms of others . . . . Water which does not flow becomes stagnant . . . . To live is to renew oneself . . . . We must emphasize the fact that the firm is a peculiar entity in permanent process of evolutionary change: it must renew and revitalize itself at all times due to the inevitable consequences of the changing technology and economy of our world.

How, then, could this be contextualized within an overall Basque setting?

Building on Basque culture and context

In reviewing the history of the Basque people, one might speak of their "associative tendencies". *They manifest strong ethnic pride and commitment*

Table 10.1 Social economy and cooperative enterprise

Innovation driven institutionalized research: researcher The social economy: social economics to cooperative enterprise

- *Communal attributes*: <u>Grounding</u> – Constituting Africa, Sekem Commonwealth, European Compass; <u>Emergence</u> – social research paradigm, social ecology, integral development; <u>Navigation</u> – communitalism, integral university, reinventing knowledge; <u>Effect</u> – *social economy*, knowledge creation, solidarity economy.
- *Integrator role*: Researcher and innovator, e.g. *Father Arizmendiarrietta*.
- *Research function*: scholarship, research and knowledge creation via *social economics and cooperative enterprise*.
- *Navigating knowledge creation*: institutionalized research *grounded in the sovereignty of labour* and subordination of capital; is embodied in *social economics and the socialization of knowledge*; emerging collaboration of three main agents – *universities, technology centers and companies;* ultimately leading *social transformation*; *culminating in a cooperatively based social economy in the Basque country.*

to egalitarian values and democratic governance. And they believe in the dignity of labour (Whyte and Whyte, 1991). In the sixteenth and seventeenth centuries, every male head of a family in the Basque country was entitled to vote for members of the municipal government. The Basque guilds, at the same time, were health and welfare organizations, as well as units of production. They protected their workers and helped orphans and widows, and they opened hospitals. They formed networks of skilled workers, which bid for jobs, distributed the work among the guilds, and delivered the finished products. Although the guilds lost their monopoly powers when large industry developed, the guild tradition survived in the region.

At the same time, in overall scale and scope today, the Mondragon complex is unique in the Basque country and the world.

The development of Mondragon

Development in phases

The formative years in the history of the Mondragon complex, then, began with their projects in community health, the building of a sports program, and particularly, as indicated, the campaign to establish the school in the 1950s. In the continuing dialogues with Don Jose Maria the founders learned the importance of integrating into their social vision a high level of competence in technical and economic affairs. *This linking of social, economic and technological ideas was important not only in shaping the internal development of each cooperative, but in beginning the development of a network of mutually supportive ones.*

The development of the Mondragon Cooperatives falls into two phases: the establishment of the Ulgor steel foundry, and the many cooperatives that followed, over the course of the next 35 years, and the more closely integrated Mondragon Cooperative Corporation (MCC) in 1991. The basic building blocks of MCC are its industrial cooperatives owned and operated by its workers. They share in the profits or losses of the business according to the work value of their jobs, and have an equal say in its governance. That they are able to do this is due to the unique structures and systems of governance that the Mondragon Cooperatives have developed.

Unique structures and systems

The General Assembly is the highest authority. The Governing Council conducts the affairs of the cooperative. Council meetings are held before the working day begins. The manager may attend in an advisory capacity, but has no vote. There is a separate Management Council where the top executives meet. So governance and operations are clearly separated. The final body, the annually selected Social Council, represents primarily the workers. Built into it is the union function: "From the point of view of membership, we are all represented in the Governing Council, but if that were the only organ of representation, our participation in the firm would be very little, at least regarding the ordinary matters of working life. To avoid the passivity and facilitate direct experience with many problems we brought the Social Council into existence" (Whyte and Whyte, 1991).

The Caja Laboral as a social and economic laboratory

Stakeholding and democratic governance apart, the success of the Mondragon Cooperatives is also largely due to the unique system of secondary or support cooperatives from which the primary cooperatives (manufacturing and retailing) source key specialist services. Arizmendi realized at a very early stage in the life of the cooperatives that expanding the existing businesses and creating new ones would require reliable access to capital on affordable terms. "A cooperative", he wrote, "must not condemn itself to the sole alternative of self-financing". His insight led, in 1959, to *the establishment of the Caja in order to mobilize capital from the local and regional communities, and to act as a kind of social and economic laboratory.* It was to become not only the financer but also the driving force in shaping development and in holding the cooperatives together.

From functioning purely as a source of capital for the cooperatives, the Caja then moved on to become the mechanism through which their association with one another was formalized and their activities integrated. Each cooperative was required to invest in the Caja, including holdings on behalf of the members, such as pension funds and workers' share capital. Each cooperative was required to adopt a five-year budget and report on it at monthly intervals.

Finally, the Caja had a key role in developing new cooperatives, as well as advising and helping out existing cooperatives that were experiencing difficulties. These latter services were performed by the Caja Laboral as "factory factory". The division consisted of seven departments: advice and consultation; feasibility studies; agricultural and food promotion; industrial promotion; intervention; urban planning and building; auditing and information. Where new cooperatives were concerned, a group of workers who were interested in establishing a new venture had first to find a product or service for which they believed there was a market, along with a manager. They were then in a position to approach the so-called Business Division of the Caja. If approved, the "godfather" continued to be seconded until a break-even point was reached. The Division continued to remain in touch through the monthly reporting. Finance then aside, knowledge has played a fundamental part in Mondragon's evolution.

Knowledge creation and R & D are key

For Jose Maria Aldecoa, in fact, a recent President of Mondragon's "consejo general", *Mondragon's knowledge orientation, with its own university, is what "makes us stand out as a business group."* He continues,

> The knowledge industry in which it operates, is, next to finance, industry and distribution, the fourth product area of the Group. The university offers engineering and management degrees, alongside studies of humanities and education, including teacher training and psycho-pedagogy. It is worth noting that *the research model, which the university is pursuing, is a collaborative one, carried out with the collaboration of three main agents: universities, technology centers and companies.* (Azurmendi, 1984)

We now turn to organizational culture.

Organizational culture and cooperative knowledge

Framework and systems

To understand Mondragon, we need to understand its organizational culture, including the support system that maintains that culture and influences its ability to change in adaptive ways. In their book *Making Mondragon*, William and Katherine Whyte think of the culture of the Mondragon Cooperatives in terms of two concept categories: the cognitive framework and the shaping systems. *The cognitive framework is the set of ideas and beliefs about basic values, organizational objectives and guiding principles that from the foundation of any organization. Shaping systems enable an organization to be maintained or to change.* A culture does not maintain itself but is shaped by forces such as major policies, structures, and instruments of governance and management, starting out with the Mondragon philosophy.

Mondragon philosophy

Equality: All human beings in the Mondragon context are deemed to have been created equal, with equal rights and obligations.

Solidarity: Members of a given cooperative should rise and fall together; this principle also applies to relationships between cooperatives, and between Mondragon and the Basque community.

Dignity of labour: There should be integrity to any labour, blue or white collar.

Participation: Members have the right and obligation to participate as much as possible in shaping the decisions that affect them.

We are now ready to conclude.

Conclusion: cooperative remaking of economics

Economic capital and social cohesion

In the final analysis, for contemporary American Catholic social philosopher John Medaille, *Mondragon's success proves that there is no inherent contradiction between justice and good business* (Medaille, 2007). People despair of finding a solution to our current economic and social chaos because they confuse social "reality" with a natural one. Cut-throat globalization is not "real" in the latter sense. Nor is it permanent. Indeed, the process is so destabilizing that it will either find a way to heal itself or else it will collapse into chaos and war, a process that seems to be happening before our eyes. Healing the wounds of globalization will require the application of the principles we have dealt with so far, and will require both social and technological innovation, as has evidently been the case at Mondragon.

Mondragon as an effectively institutionalized genealogy

Finally, reflecting on the Mondragon phenomenon from a micro- and macro-economic perspective, we can see, genealogically, how the Basque *community*, mediated through what we might term a "one man *sanctuary*", Father Arizmendiarrietta, in the middle of the last century, gave rise to what, in the early days, turned out to be a major, *experimental laboratory*, in cooperativism. Subsequently also linked with an adjacent *research university*, the Mondragon cooperative movement has become world renowned.

In that respect, what we are saying is that such an inter-institutional genealogy is not necessarily restricted to what we have typecast as a structural equivalent of innovation driven, institutionalized research, but that the four constituents – community, sanctuary, university and laboratory – can vary by degree, each in turn, depending on the overall integral orientation, whether for example economic or educational in their overall approach. Arizmendi started out with education and ended by focusing, in particular, on enterprise. As we shall now see, via the knowledge creating enterprise, we have another variation on this integral theme, one less "southern" and more "eastern" in nature and scope. As such we turn, in the next chapter, to the "eastern" path of renewal leading to the Japanese knowledge creating company; that is, from macro social economy to micro knowledge creating enterprise, and from the European "south" to the far "east".

References

Azurmendi, J. (1984) *El Hombre Cooperative: Pensamiento de Jose Maria Arizmendiarrieta.* London: Sage.

Freire, P. (2000) *Pedagogy of the Oppressed.* London: Continuum.

Maritain, J. (1996) *Integral Humanism, Freedom in the Modern World, and a Letter on Independence,* Collected Works of Jacques Maritain, eds Bird, O. and O'Sullivan, R. Notre Dame, IN: University of Notre Dame Press.

Medaille, J. (2007) *The Vocation of Business: Social Justice and the Marketplace.* London: Continuum.

Mondragon Corporation (2012) http://www.mondragon-corporation.com/eng/ (accessed May 2012).

Mounier, E. (1989) *Personalism.* Notre Dame, IN: University of Notre Dame Press.

Whyte, W. and Whyte, K. (1991) *Making Mondragon.* Ithaca, NY: Cornell University Press.

11 Knowledge creation
Operations to knowledge creation

Summary of chapter:

1 knowledge has a grounded origination in a knowledge and value base;
2 it emerges middle–up–down through knowledge practitioners, knowledge officers and especially knowledge engineers – as project managers;
3 it is navigated through a hierarchical business or academic functional system;
4 it is effected via a networked, autonomous and interdependent project layer;
5 all this culminates in a knowledge creating enterprise.

Introduction: the renewal path of navigation

Transforming operations, technology and competence

We now turn from the social economy, the "southern" (in European terms) relational effect of innovation driven institutionalized research, functionally, and such an effective institutional genealogy, structurally, to the knowledge creating company, involving a now "eastern" renewal effect (Lessem and Schieffer, 2009). As such we turn from the Spanish Basque country, ultimately to Japan, whereby, at least at the end of the last century, a developmental approach to knowledge creation transcended an analytical approach to managing operations. Thereby, such an approach to recognizing individual competence, managing an enterprise's operations and applying technology is replaced by overall knowledge creation, for us an enterprise variation on the theme of innovation driven research as per *CARE* and institutional genealogy as per CARE.

There has been lots of talk on knowledge management and knowledge creation in the past decades. However, as we see it, the Achilles heel of

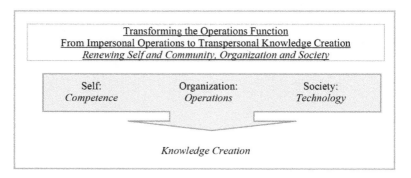

Figure 11.1 Transforming the operations function.

the new move towards a so-called "knowledge based society", is that such a typically "north-western" approach does not build on prior grounds of "southern" community building, and on "eastern" conscious evolution. Once again the north and the west dominate over the rest, which results in a technical and economic "north-western" pre-emphasis, over and above nature and culture, drawing relatively more on the "south-east".

In other words, we need to transform technology, operations and competence in a knowledge creating light, as intimated in the last chapter through the case of Mondragon, and further reinforced in this one. Indeed, one of the reasons why so-called "knowledge management" today is so dominated by technology, is that the more social and cultural influence in this area, serving as such to build on our *integral realms*, that came from Japan, has waned, and the influence of the south, embodied in so-called indigenous knowledge systems that are deeply rooted in nature and culture, has been minimal.

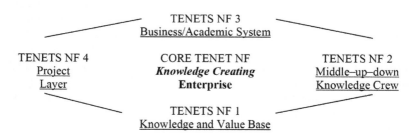

Figure 11.2 Knowledge effect: institutional R & D – renewal.

Homo faber to information technology

That having been said, the progressive transformation of materially based operations into information-based knowledge systems has probably been more marked than in any other of the functional cases, and this is down, in no small way, to the influence of Japan especially in the latter part of the last century. Actually, the only other major function that was added to marketing, human resources and finance, over the course of a whole century, has been information technology, as an adjunct of operations.

It was also the operational function alone, which was significantly influenced by a culture and society outside of the "west" and "north", that is by the "east" in the specific guise of Japan. In fact it was this fusion of "Japanese Spirit–Western Technique" that gave rise to the new push towards organizational learning and development. We now turn to the transformative journey from operations to knowledge creation, starting on the "northern-eastern" ground", that is, with Karl Popper's open society, and then moving "east" towards a knowledge creating Japan.

Northern–eastern grounding and emergence

Grounding and origination: the open society

The term "open society", which serves to ground the European "northeast", was first significantly evolved by Austrian immigrant to the UK, the research philosopher Karl Popper, as originator of "critical rationalism". Popper argued in his book *Open Society and its Enemies* (1977) that open society is threatened by universal ideologies, like capitalism and socialism, that claim to be in possession of the ultimate truth. Both Karl Popper and his follower, philosopher and financier George Soros, escaped from a totalitarian system. Whereas Popper, a Jew, had to flee to England from Nazi Austria, Hungarian-born George Soros, also Jewish, had to flee from communist Eastern Europe to the UK and thereafter to the USA (Soros, 2000). While Popper became one of the pre-eminent philosophers of our time, Soros became a noted international financier, philosopher as well as philanthropist. Both Popper and Soros were born and bred in Eastern Europe, that is, respectively in Austria and Hungary.

We now turn from Austria and Hungary to Catalonia.

Emergence and foundation: network society – the net and the self

Manuel Castells is a Catalonian–Spanish sociologist, currently resident both in Spain and in the west coast of America. In his recent trilogy, which culminated in *The End of Millennium*, he focused in particular on the emerging "network society" in contrast to the formerly industrialized one, whereby he stressed:

> *By industrialism I mean a mode of development in which the main sources of productivity are not the quantitative increases of factors of production – labour, capital and natural resources – together with the use of new sources of energy. Rather, by informationalism I mean a mode of development in which the main source of productivity is the qualitative capacity to optimise the combination and use of factors of production on the basis of knowledge and information. The last quarter of the 20th century has been therefore marked by the transition from industrialism to statism, and from the industrial society to the network society.* (Castells, 2009)

This emerging technological and organizational development, arising out of an open society, sets the stage for what is to follow. In fact a new world, for Castells, is taking shape at the end of the last millennium. It originates in the historical coincidence around the late 1960s and mid-1970s of three independent processes: the information technology revolution; the economic crisis of both capitalism and statism, and their subsequent restructuring; and the blooming of cultural social movements, such as libertarianism, human rights, feminism and environmentalism. *The interaction between these technological and cultural processes and the reactions they triggered brought into being a new dominant social structure: the network society; a new economy; the informational, global economy; and a new culture, the culture of real virtuality.* The logic embedded in this economy and society underlies all institutions in an interdependent world. Particularly important is IT's role in allowing the development of networking as a dynamic, self-expanding form or organization of humanity. This prevailing networking logic transforms all domains of social and economic life.

For Castells, therefore, societies today are constituted of the interaction between the global "net" and the local "self", the global technologically laden network society and the local power of psychological identity. Yet unless the two – in our terms the global exogenous and local indigenous – are fused together, the former serves to fragment rather than to reconstitute society. People's experience remains confined to simple, segregated locales, while global elites, be they Facebook's Zuckerberg or Google's Larry Page and Sergey Brin, retrench within immaterial (if not also material) palaces made up of communication networks and information flows. *Therefore a long march is required from communities built around local resistance identity to the heights of new local as well as global project identities, sprouting from the values nurtured in these. For this transition from resistance to project identity, a new politics will need to emerge.* This will be a cultural politics that connects to values and experiences that spring from local people's life experience, while simultaneously connecting up with global issues and development.

As we move from such an emerging economy and society towards the kind of institution that arises from it, we come, again, but now in more "northern-eastern" guise, upon Nonaka and Takeuchi's knowledge creating enterprise. In such, network transcends hierarchy, in the newly normed "hypertext organization", as a further, organizational evolution of Castells' "network society". Working with and through knowledge in a fundamentally new fashion transcends employment per se, via a "knowledge crew", set within a knowledge creating enterprise.

North-eastern navigation and effect: knowledge creating enterprise

Enterprise renewal: knowledge creation to continuous innovation

Nonaka and Takeuchi then maintain that the path taken by a knowledge creating enterprise is, in essence, to turn knowledge creation into continuous innovation, aligned functionally for us with innovation driven research (though for Nonaka more often than not technologically based research), as well as

Table 11.1 Knowledge creation and organizational renewal

Effect of innovation driven institutionalized research: renewal path The knowledge creating enterprise Knowledge base to project layer

- *Communal attributes*: Grounding – Constituting Africa, Sekem Commonwealth, European Compass; Emergence – social research paradigm, social ecology, integral development; Navigation – communitalism, integral university, reinventing knowledge; Effect – social economy, *knowledge creation*, solidarity economy.
- *Integrator role*: institutionalized research, e.g. *Nonaka, Takeuchi*.
- *Research function*: scholarship, research and knowledge creation in *hypertext organization*.
- Navigating knowledge creation: grounded origination in a *knowledge and value base*; emerging *middle–up–down* through knowledge practitioners, knowledge officers and especially **knowledge engineers**; navigated through an *hierarchical business or academic functional system*; effected through a *networked, autonomous and interdependent project layer*; culminating in a *knowledge creating enterprise*.

a new institutional genealogy of sorts, structurally, so as to gain subsequent comparative advantage. A first step for a knowledge creating enterprise, functionally then, is to define the "field" or "domain" that gives a mental map of the world in which, for example, a Canon or Sony lives, and provide a general direction regarding what kind of knowledge they ought to seek to create.

Most organizations only have products and services in mind when formulating strategy. Such products and services have clear boundaries. In contrast, boundaries for knowledge are more obscure, helping to expand the organization's economic, technological and social scope. A case in point, for example, is Matsushita's knowledge-based vision in 1990:

- We are in the "human innovation business", a business that creates new lifestyles based on creativity, comfort and joy in addition to efficiency and convenience.
- We produce "humanware technology", technology based on human studies such as artificial intelligence, fuzzy logic, neuro-computers, networking technology.

Nonaka and Takeuchi identify three key "enabling conditions" for the knowledge creating enterprise, which for us are closely aligned with innovation driven, institutionalized research, albeit Nonaka's focus is on technological innovation:

- First, develop intentionally the organizational *capability to acquire, create, accumulate and exploit knowledge*;
- second, *build up autonomous individuals and groups*, setting their task boundaries by themselves to pursue the ultimate intention of the organization;
- third, provide employees with *a sense of crisis – as well as a lofty ideal* – as such so-called "creative chaos" increases tension within the organization.

How, then, does the so-called "hypertext" organization, which brings us on to our institutional genealogy, as we shall soon see, serve to promote such organizational renewal, and overall knowledge networking, as well as, for us, serving to transformatively effect innovation driven, institutionalized research?

The hypertext organization

The project layer: laboratory orientation

Nonaka refers to a "hypertext" organization, because of its layered nature and scope, which serves to develop, channel and distribute knowledge through the duly formed networks. The top stratum of this kind of enterprise comprises the "project team" layer (see Figure 11.3), as per a research or learning laboratory. Multiple project teams engage in knowledge creating activities such as new product and systems development. In all such cases the team members are brought together from, and networked across, a number of different units throughout the business system, and are assigned exclusively to a project team until the project is completed.

The bureaucratic system: research university

Alongside this project layer, but occupying a lower order of knowledge creating significance, is the conventional "bureaucratic system" – in our case constituted of academic departments – with its normal hierarchy of authority. The project layer, on the one hand, is engaged with developing new knowledge through self-organizing groups. The hierarchical system, on the other, is primarily concerned with categorizing, ordering, distributing and commercializing or operationalizing such knowledge. In terms of Nonaka and Takeuchi's knowledge spiral (SECI) introduced in our earlier volume, *Awakening Integral Consciousness*, whereas the project layer is primarily focused upon "southern" Socialization and "eastern" Externalization, the hierarchical system is more engaged with "northern" Combination and "western" Internalization. Underlying both project layer and business system, for Nonaka and Takeuchi, is a "knowledge foundation".

The knowledge foundations: sanctuary

This third layer does not exist as an actual organizational entity, but is embedded in corporate vision, organizational culture, and technology. Of course, in our context here, societal culture is of even greater significance than the corporate one. *The vision arises from these spiritual, aesthetic and scientific knowledge grounds. If made explicit, it provides the direction in which the enterprise should develop its social as well as technological innovations.* Moreover, it clarifies the overall "field" in which it wants to play, for us in moral and aesthetic as well as scientific–technological terms. Furthermore, while vision and culture provide the experiential and imaginal base to tap tacit knowledge, technology taps the explicit knowledge generated in the other two layers.

A knowledge creating enterprise ultimately must have the organizational ability to acquire, accumulate, exploit and create knowledge continuously and dynamically. Moreover it must be able to recategorize and recontextualize it strategically for use by others in the organization or by future generations. As Nonaka and Takeuchi have indicated, a hierarchy is the

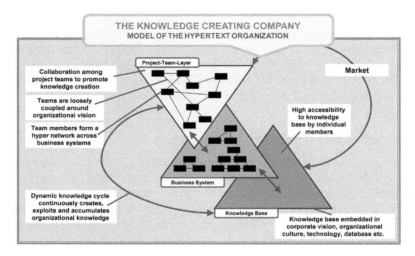

Figure 11.3 The hypertext organization.

most efficient structure for the acquisition, accumulation and exploitation of knowledge, while a task force is the most effective for the creation of new knowledge.

We now turn to the so-called "knowledge crew", as opposed to conventional managers and employees, who run such a hypertext organization.

The knowledge crew

What is seldom recognized is the way in which Nonaka and Takeuchi have dissolved the notion of "labour", or even, if you like, "people as our greatest asset", and replaced these terms with knowledge creators. *Such a transformation from "labour" to knowledge is distinctly absent from the "western" literature on knowledge management, which is much more strongly rooted in technology.* For the Japanese organizational sociologists there are three kinds of knowledge creators, or researcher-and-innovators: knowledge practitioners, knowledge engineers, knowledge officers.

Knowledge practitioners

Knowledge practitioners consist of "knowledge operators" like technicians, who interface with tacit knowledge for the most part, and "knowledge specialists" like computer programmers, who interface primarily with explicit knowledge. *Such practitioners develop a strongly personal perspective, a strong degree of openness to discussion and debate, as well as a variety of experiences inside and outside the organization from and through which they are able to learn.* They also acquire a high degree of specific skill-based competence, and functional management knowledge, as well as expertise in interacting with colleagues and customers.

Knowledge engineers

Knowledge engineers, constituting the heart of the knowledge creating enterprise, are responsible for converting tacit knowledge into explicit knowledge and vice versa, thereby facilitating the four modes of knowledge creation. As such *they mediate between the "what should be" mindset of the senior management and the "what is" mindset of the frontline employees by creating mid-level business and product concepts.* Such middle managers synthesize the tacit knowledge of both frontline employees and executives, make it explicit, and incorporate it into new products and technologies. Such knowledge engineers become proficient in employing metaphors and in developing storylines, to help themselves and others imagine the future. They become adept at communication whereby they encourage dialogue, and grow their competence in developing new strategic concepts. *They are able to develop methodologies for knowledge creation, and become equipped with project management capabilities.*

Knowledge officers

Knowledge officers, finally, are responsible for managing the total knowledge creation process at the organizational level. They are, therefore, expected to give an enterprise's knowledge creating activities a sense of direction by articulating grand concepts – like sustainable development – on what the organization might be, establishing a knowledge vision in the form of a policy statement, and setting the standards for justifying the value of the knowledge that is being created. In other words, *knowledge officers are responsible for articulating the company's "conceptual umbrella", the grand concepts that in highly universal and abstract terms identify the common features linking disparate business activities into a coherent whole.* In short, knowledge officers direct the entire process of knowledge creation. They create chaos within the project team, setting challenging goals for would-be leaders, and they have responsibility for selecting the right project leaders or knowledge engineers in key areas. Finally, they interact with team members on a hands-on basis and solicit commitment from them.

Conclusion: towards knowledge creation

Transformative effect

In concluding this "north-eastern" chapter, we have focused on the transformative effect of innovation driven institutionalized research, or indeed knowledge creation, coupled with an institutional genealogy most especially focused on the knowledge creating enterprise. Such an enterprise, be it a Sony or a Honda, was conceived of and effected most prolifically among large-scale manufacturing enterprises in Japan, that is, until the demise of the "Japanese economic miracle", at the turn of the millennium.

We locate then such enterprise renewal as: *Grounded origination in a knowledge and value base; emerging middle–up–down through knowledge practitioners, knowledge officers and especially knowledge engineers; navigated through a hierarchical business or academic functional system; effected via a networked, autonomous and interdependent project layer; culminating in a knowledge creating enterprise.*

Table 11.2 The integral path of renewal

Releasing the GENE-ius of the northern-eastern function *Evolving operations into knowledge creation through a fourfold process*	
The north-eastern GENE	*Core criteria for integral enterprise*
Grounding: Community The northern function is grounded in an *open society.*	• accommodating fallibility/ reflexivity • openness towards new economic, financial and political architectures
Emerging: Sanctuary From there it emerges through *communications networks . . .*	• from separate material factors to inter-connected communications systems • capacity to optimize on the basis of knowledge and information
Navigating: Academy . . . gives rise to a *knowledge creating enterprise.*	• build up knowledge crews: knowledge officer, engineer and practitioner • develop knowledge vision / enable conditions for knowledge creation
Effecting: Laboratory Finally, it becomes fully effective through a wide degree of knowledge sharing, ultimately through *Networked Knowledge.*	• "You cannot control a resource" • a project layer provides a space for freedom and self-organization

In Table 11.2, as illustrated above, we have visually distilled the overall argument, and also aligned it with our institutional genealogy. In essence, then, while knowledge creation for Nonaka and Takeuchi is largely aligned with technological, as opposed to *social*, innovation, as organizational sociologists their major focus is on social means to that end. Moreover, and harking back to our genealogy, as per Chapter 9, the *knowledge creating company* not only becomes a veritable *laboratory*, but arguably creates more new knowledge, as such, than the conventional *university*. Moreover, not only does such knowledge creation build on prior *community*, but, in a technological sense, as per Castells, information and communications technology becomes a *virtual* religion, as an *open source sanctuary,* so to speak.

We are now finally ready to turn from the path of renewal to that of reasoned realization, duly aligning in this unique societal case, institutionalized research and the solidarity economy, as per the "north-west", ironically represented here, as we shall see, by Brazil in *South* America.

References

Castells, M. (2009) *The Rise of the Network Society*. Chichester: Wiley-Blackwell.

Lessem, R. and Schieffer, A. (2009) *Transformation Management: Towards the Integral Enterprise*. Abingdon: Routledge.

Nonaka, I. and Takeuchi, H. (1995) *The Knowledge Creating Company*. Oxford: Oxford University Press.

Popper, K. (1977) *Open Society and its Enemies*. Abingdon: Routledge.

Soros, G. (2000) *Open Society: Reforming Global Capitalism*. New York: Little, Brown.

12 Solidarity economy
Comparative to integral advantage in Brazil

Summary of chapter:

1 institutionalized research is grounded in the eco-services of the rainforest;
2 it emerges in "mestizo logic" – cultural democracy reversing cultural imperialism;
3 it is navigated via the new science of "Tropicology", the Paulisto School of Sociology and CEBRAP, the Brazilian Center for Analysis and Planning, whereby development is measured by the quality of attention a country gives to its people and its culture;
4 it is ultimately effected by reimagining trade via experimentation with institutions, ideas, techniques coupled with questioning our shared institutional assumptions.

Introduction: the effect of the path of reasoned realization

Revisiting emerging markets and societies

In this concluding chapter, now concerning the effect of innovation driven, institutionalized Research from the vantage point of reasoned realization, we turn, perhaps surprisingly, to Brazil. In my recent book *Integral Advantage: Revisiting Emerging Markets and Societies*, duly applied to the BRICS countries, I positioned Brazil, geographically and ontologically so to speak, in the "south-west" (Lessem, 2015). Recent experience (as of August 2016) of the Rio Olympic Games may serve to bear this out. However, notwithstanding its strongly *relational* credentials, there is, additionally, a path of *reasoned realization* that this hybrid "mestizo" country has prominently followed, at least in recent years.

Specifically moreover, and in reviewing Brazil's GENE-ius as such, we have pursued what we have termed *integral advantage* from the perspective of nature, culture, social science and market economy. Indeed, we would argue that the country's political and economic troubles of late are because it has not pursued such an integral path of reasoned realization, consistently, building on what has come relationally and renewal wise before, consciously.

From comparative advantage to taking CARE

To begin with as such, we remind ourselves of the theory of *comparative advantage*, originated by David Ricardo in the nineteenth century, and cited by founder of the BRICS concept, Goldman Sachs' Jim O'Neil (2011), that underlies today's conventional wisdom on "emerging markets", as per the so-called BRICS countries – Brazil, Russia, India, China, South Africa – in the twenty-first century, altogether aligned with economic growth:

> *unrestricted exchange between countries will increase total world output if each country specializes in those goods it can produce at a <u>relatively</u> lower cost compared to its potential trading partners. Each country will then trade some of its lower-cost goods for others that can be produced elsewhere more cheaply than at home. <u>With free trade among nations, all countries will find that their consumption possibilities have been expanded by such specialization and trade beyond that what would have been possible from their domestic production possibilities alone.</u> Because of this compelling argument, economists tend to favor free trade, since it is presumed to be "welfare enhancing" in that the aggregate level of world income is increased ....*

I have paraphrased the above, as if we were pursuing <u>integral</u> advantage, thereby *CARE* (see bold lettering below)-ing-4-Society as a whole:

> <u>exchange and reconciliation within and between countries</u> *will increase <u>local and global wellbeing if each country pursues its natural, cultural, social and economic advantage thereby exchanging knowledge and value</u> with its potential trading partners, thus reimagining free trade. With such <u>exchange and reconciliation</u> among nations, <u>specific local Communities are activated within particular countries, within which integral consciousness is **A**wakened, as a sanctified whole, whereby and thereafter innovation driven technological and social **R**esearch is duly institutionalized academy wise, and transformatively **E**mbodied laboratory wise within and across each. Through such each country will actualize its individual societal uniqueness and thereby contribute</u>*

to the integrated potential of the global whole. We favour as such the pursuit of each country's integral advantage, since it is presumed to be "welfare enhancing" in that the aggregate level of local and global wellbeing is thereby increased.

We shall now journey through Brazil's potential, if not also actual, GENE-ius, thereby bringing our Institutional Genealogy to social and economic life, in a particular country, in pursuit of would-be integral advantage, with a particular focus on the effect of innovation driven, institutionalized research, starting on the ground with nature, as the integral starting point, or grounding, of such.

Natural and local Brazilian grounding in community

The rainforest was her people's life

Marina Silva, 2014 Presidential candidate in Brazil, as described in the book by her American follower, Ziporah Hildebrandt (2001), had originally grown up in the *seringal*, the rubber-tapping region of Amazonia. The rainforest was her people's life. They loved their trees as friends and relatives. *Marina*, already as a young child, *dreamed that her people would be recognized for their character and their knowledge of the forest, rather than scorned for their poverty and illiteracy.* In our terms such "knowledge of forest" is the source of *relational* research origination, albeit not yet formally *reason-and-realization-wise* institutionalized.

Forest people and communities would then control their own lives rather than suffering under the brutal power of wealthy ranchers, businesspeople and politicians. At school Marina learned about both liberation theology and the educational methods of Paulo Freire. *Libration theology showed*

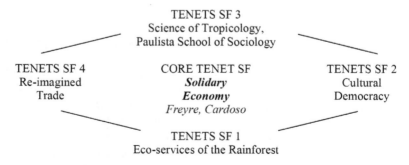

Figure 12.1 Effect of Brazilian institutional R & D: reasoned.

Marina how her burning need to understand God, herself and the world, could build on her grandmother's simple morals, and expand into a vision of justice and equality. Her own research, then, started with physical, and developed as human, nature.

Carrying the dream to the government

In 1990 Marina was ultimately elected representative to Acre's state congress. She was incredibly popular with the poor of Acre. There was nobody like her, for Hildebrandt: a rubber tapper, born poor as they were, with a university degree. More miraculous was the fact that Marina had not forgotten her good fortune.

She in fact called herself "the tip of the iceberg", in that, *"I am the voice and fight of so many who are against the destruction of the Amazon, but who are in favor of developing it with sensitivity to its eco-structure and awareness of its impact on so many lives. This is why I became a senator".* Once she was in the senate, *Marina Silva's mission was to change how Brazil – and the world – thought about Amazonia: not as a place to exploit, but as a resource to care (our CARE) for*; not as an empty space, but as home to millions of people and to the species of a priceless ecosystem, and, in our terms, as the grounding for innovative research.

Over 70 per cent of drugs, for example, are derived from plants that come from Amazonia. Researchers believe that cures for diseases like cancer, AIDS and heart disease are hidden in tropical forests, and many a pharmaceutical company's innovation driven institutionalized research would be founded on this, but as a basis for scientific and technological (medical), rather than social, innovation. Yet indigenous nations as opposed to exogenous companies, Marina argued, now with her newly acquired political status, get none of the profits. *"One fungus, one plant or insect could produce a product worth millions or billions of dollars. A portion of that money, returned to rainforest communities, would support sustainable development in Amazonia".*

"When I really dream I think we should come up with solutions to show the world," Marina Silva has said (Hildebrandt, 2001). *With its vast rainforest, traditional peoples and high technology, Brazil could become a world leader by showing a new vision of society working with nature.* For her, innovation driven, institutionalized research should be grounded in communities, rather than be merely exploited by corporations. We now turn to Gilbert Freyre to take the Brazilian natural and communal local story on, now culturally and societally, via historians Peter Burke and Maria Lucia Pallares Burke, both based at Cambridge University in England, thereby locally (Maria Lucia Pallares Burke) and globally (Peter Burke) (Burke and Pallares-Burke, 2006).

Luso-Tropicology: local–global emergent Brazilian sanctuary

Mestizo logic: towards a racial democracy

Gilberto Freyre was born in Recife – as indeed his namesake Paulo Freire was – in the Brazilian North-East in 1900 (he died in 1987). He travelled around Europe and America in his young adulthood, and became a veritable polymath – historian, anthropologist, sociologist, politician and journalist – over the rest of his twentieth-century life. In his best-known work *Masters and Slaves*, written in the 1950s, *instead of equating the mixture of races with deterioration, he associated it with the improvement of species* (Freyre, 1974).

Although Freyre preferred the anthropological approach, as such, with its emphasis on the direct observation and the details of everyday life, he was more involved with sociology, a subject on which he was to write a textbook. He regularly used terms from sociology, such as "sub-culture", or "social cohesion", or the idea of a "complex".

Notable for the Burkes, moreover, is Freyre's polemic against abstraction and quantitative methods, to which he prefers impressionistic descriptions

Table 12.1 Solidarity economy

Innovation driven institutionalized research: researcher The solidarity economy: eco-services to market and institutional experimentation
• *Communal attributes*: <u>Grounding</u> – Constituting Africa, Sekem Commonwealth, European creativity; <u>Emergence</u> – integral paradigm, integral genealogy, integral university; <u>Navigation</u> – Pundutso (Zimbabwe), Ciser/ACIRD (Nigeria), Citizen's Initiative (Slovenia); <u>Effect</u> – social economy, knowledge creation, *solidarity economy*. • *Integrator role*: researcher and innovator, e.g. ***Marina Silva, Gilberto Freire, Fernando Cardoso, Mangabeira Unger***. • *Research function*: scholarship, research and knowledge creation via <u>social economics and cooperative enterprise</u>. • *Navigating knowledge creation*: institutionalized research grounded in the ***eco-services of the rainforest***; emerging through ***"mestizo logic" in terms of cultural democracy*** reversing cultural imperialism; navigated via the new ***Science of "Tropicology"***, at Instituto Nabuco in Recife, the ***Paulisto School of Sociology*** and ***CEBRAP*** the Brazilian Centre for Analysis and Planning in Sao Paulo whereby true development is measured by the quality of attention the country gives to its people and its culture; ultimately effected by re-imagining trade through ***restless experimentation with institutions, ideas and techniques*** coupled with the ***ability to question and revise our shared institutional and imaginative assumptions.***

packed with concrete and sensuous details. *Sociology*, he maintained, *should be "polytheist" rather than "monotheist"*. *"It has to be mixed and amphibious concerned with natures and cultures"*. Sociology, for him, depends on its neighbours: anthropology, ecology, social history, folklore, psychoanalysis, biology and other disciplines. People on the margins of the profession, for example journalists and historians, had a fundamental contribution to make.

His own writings are an attempt to mediate, then, between art and science, sociology and literature, insider and outsider, involvement and attachment, intuition and analysis, of, if you like, a "mestizo logic".

Cultural imperialism in reverse

According to Freyre, therefore, it was easier for the Portuguese than for the British or Dutch to survive in the tropics because so far as climate is concerned, *Portugal "is more Africa than Europe"*. This "acclimatability" was accompanied by an adaptability to local customs. "Tropicalism", for him then, is worth taking seriously. It describes a project intended to combat what Freyre calls "the persistent notion that everything tropical is the negation of the refinement of civilization". At a more general level, Freyre suggested that Brazil might become a leader in the process of making "civilized man in cold regions" aware of the aesthetic values of the tropics. He *predicted a movement that might be described as cultural imperialism in reverse, with the tropics leading and Europe following, not least because Brazil was a pioneer in racial mixing that had become characteristic of the world in the twentieth century.*

Tropicalism to solidarity economics: navigation via university

Tropicalism as a new science

The new science of tropicology in fact found a home in the institute Freyre helped to found, the *Instituto Nabuco* in Recife. How, then, might Freyre be viewed in an international context? We now turn most specifically, in the context of innovation driven institutionalized research, with a view to its effect on politics and economics, from Gilberto Freyre to Brazil's former president, and fellow sociologist, the internationally renowned Fernando Cardoso.

Paulista School of Sociology

Mauricio Font is the Director of the Bildner Center for Western Hemisphere Studies at CUNY University, New York, and editor of *Charting a New*

Course, based on the work of Fernando Cardoso (2001). Cardoso was unique in transforming himself from an academic sociologist in the 1970s into Brazil's President, in the 1990s, without losing touch with his sociological roots. He was thus eminently placed to turn institutionalized research into social innovation.

Already in the 1920s, Sao Paulo, where Cardoso was based (born in 1931 and became President in 1995), had become the main locus of Brazilian industrialization, economic development and modernization. But the revolution of 1930, heralding the demise of the old republic and the onset of the Vargas military dictatorship, put into question the state's pre-eminence. *A new, modern university, though, would prepare a new intellectual elite to help face this challenge. A contingent of French social scientists helped launch the social science program of the University of Sao Paulo*, among those being the exogenous French anthropologist Claude Levi-Strauss as well as the renowned historian Fernand Braudel. The key founding figure in what would be known as the *Paulista School of Sociology* was Brazil's indigenous Florestan Fernandes, Cardoso's mentor.

CESIT, CEBRAP and the invention of dependency theory

Cardoso's doctoral thesis, *Capitalism and Slavery in Southern Brazil*, provided an analysis of the rise and demise of the slavery system in the nineteenth century in the southernmost state in Brazil. His thesis approached the subject using a dense dialectical approach inspired by Karl Marx. By 1962 he had been named director of the Center for Industrial Labor Sociology (CESIT). But the 1964 military coup disrupted the Center's plans, and Cardoso fled to Chile. *Exile turned out to be a godsend.* In the social sciences and in economic thought, *Santiago in Chile may have been the intellectual capital of Latin America at the time. It provided access to a rich theoretical and comparative Latin American context* and developed frameworks through which to probe ideas about development.

While in Chile, Cardoso recast and renamed "sub-capitalism", the concept earlier developed in Sao Paulo, as the "dependent development" model. He elaborated on this in his book *Dependency and Development in Latin America* (1992). It was at this time that Cardoso met the leading American development economist Albert Hirschman, who would become a close colleague and perhaps his main influence in the US. In 1968 he decided to return to Brazil, but the fateful second denial of his academic career by the military brought Cardoso closer to the path that would eventually lead him to the Presidency. *The response to this setback was to launch CEBRAP, the Brazilian Center for Analysis and Planning, in 1969, drawing support from international foundations as well as from national sources.*

Brazilians are a solidary people

Cardoso and associates emerged as significant players in the gradual process of political reopening that began in 1973. The Brazilian Democratic Movement (MDB) was the main political organization demanding the return of democracy in the 1970s. A CEBRAP task force played a distinguished supporting role in the MDB struggle. Its very success in creating space to study alternative views about Brazilian society turned this innovative research centre and its leaders into actors in the democratic movement. Embedded in an academic and intellectual trajectory, *the Cardosian worldview accepted the leading economic role of the market, while maintaining that it does not address all needs, creates problems of its own, and tends to dissolve human solidarity.* So the state needed to play a fundamental role in reducing inequality, poverty, and other social problems.

In Cardoso's inaugural speech as President, in contrast with what the conventional BRICS wisdom implies, he said the development of a country is not measured by what it produces. *True development is measured by the quality of attention the country gives to its people and its culture.* In a world of instantaneous global communication where people fragment and specialize, *cultural identity is rooted in nations.* Brazilians, as Freyre has said, are people of great cultural heterogeneity, born from a "south-western" combination of occidental Portuguese tradition with African and indigenous Indian traditions. The collective support for the country is moved, moreover, by sentiment, and this sentiment has a name: solidarity. It lets the country break free from small circles of particular interests so that it helps its neighbour, colleague or compatriot, near or far. *Brazilians, for Cardoso, are a solidary people.*

The need for a New Renaissance

Cardoso at the same time alluded to the need for a "New Renaissance". In sum, *man today lives with the possibilities of "rebirth", a new liberty to reinvent models of social existence.* The models are still in the process of being defined, and in the present stage point more to the limits to what should not be done than to positive patterns. *Another contemporary phenomenon engendered by technical progress that reinforces the thesis of the "New Renaissance" is that of globalization, which is producing a new consciousness of the dimensions of the world.* The Renaissance established the individual as subject, and with the retreat of religious interference in politics left the terrain open for the definition of a new model of social organization, the sovereign state.

Now the advance of globalization designates "humanity as a new subject", and in a certain way, that every same state is obliged to adapt to its new circumstances. *This powerful notion of "global community" is altering our worldview.* Cardoso's compatriot, and fellow social scientist, Mangabeira Unger, takes the innovation driven, institutionalized research story on from here, towards its penultimate transformative effect.

Transformative effect: laboratory to overcome "market" fate

False necessity of "free" markets

Mangabeira Unger, based on the one hand as an academic at Harvard Law School, and on the other hand as a politician and social activist in Brazil, in his seminal work *False Necessity: Anti-Necessarian Social Theory in the Service of Radical Democracy* (2004) cited two types of fatalism that have dominated our understanding of society. One of these types is rooted in the tradition of classical European social theory from Montesquieu to Durkheim to Weber. *Marxism* has been its most relentless and influential exponent. The other type of fatalism is represented by the contemporary *positive social sciences* particularly as they have come to be practised in the universities in the United States, and has been reflected in empiricism and rationalism generally, free markets and capitalism specifically.

Such theories recognize the importance of institutions and beliefs of society. However, they *present each such formative context as an example of a general type, like capitalism or the market economy.* They see the type as an invisible system: all its elements stand or fall together. According to such a view, then, *our deliberate action is the largely unwitting agent and accessory of a historical script we are unable to rewrite.* Yet a market economy, for Mangabeira Unger, can be *effective in many different ways,* with radically different consequences for social life. Once we free ourselves from the impulse to see contemporary institutions as the outcome of a narrowing funnel of possibilities, we can begin to find in our institutional history, as Unger puts it, hidden resources for reconstruction. Two great constructive forces, then, for Mangabeira Unger in the final analysis, work upon social – including political, economic and cultural – life.

One force is restless experimentation – hence for us a "laboratory" – with institutions, ideas and techniques for the sake of enhancing our practical capabilities. This search for worldly power shades into a quest for a second, less tangible empowerment: the ability to question and revise our shared institutional and imaginative assumptions as we go about the business of life. It is the opportunity to act confidently within a society or a culture without becoming its puppets. All of this, of course, is dependent on the state of our moral development. In Mangabeira Unger's most recent book, *The Religion of the Future* (2014), he cites the axis of moral development that advances the course of our lives as a whole, ultimately reaching towards *love, in our most intimate experience,* thereby involving a sense of *community based on reciprocal engagement and recognized difference,* rather than upon similarity or sameness. From there moreover, and this is key for him, it extends to *reform of the division of labour in the spirit of the higher forms of cooperation.*

Conclusion: building a green cathedral

Natural community bereft of a social and economic laboratory

In the final analysis, then, what we see effectively being played out, through overcoming "false necessity", is the revisiting of the social solidarity, as Cardoso's means of Brazilian navigation, on the one hand, and the accommodation of difference that is such a strong theme of Freyre's emergent orientation towards hybridity, and tropicality, on the other. However, there is little harking back to origins, or standing on the grounds, as it were, of Amazonian nature, if not also local community, as per Marina Silva. Such eco-services somehow get left behind, while Brazil remains one of the most unequal – though less so than hitherto – societies on Earth, as well as being one of the most environmentally destructive (of the Amazonian rainforest). American environmentalist Juan de Onis (1992), made the point, over twenty years ago:

> *The waste of wood, natural forest products, and unique genetic resources through extensive land clearing is incalculable. The loss of potentially recoverable gold and tin, in the way these minerals are mined in Amazonia, is worth billions of dollars. Experience has shown that tropical commodities, such as coffee and cacao, carry high risks in international markets, and bulk grains are uncompetitive without a reduction of freight costs through heavy investment in agro-industrial processing in the region and a railroad system that replaces trucks. In consequence, the forests and the mineral resources must be the foundations for a new strategy of economic development of Amazonia based on productive activities that are profitable, socially stabilizing, and compatible with the life-sustaining ecosystems that are Amazonia's most valuable natural resources.*

Towards a Brazilian institutional genealogy

To that extent, Marina Silva, in defending the rainforest and its communities, and indeed, beyond such, drawing on both as the very grounds of

Brazil's pursuit of integral advantage, has a long way to go. Perhaps she needs to become the nation's next President, in place of the now discredited Dilma Roussef!

As such, and altogether: *institutionalized research will be grounded in the eco-services of the communal rainforest, emerging through a sanctified "mestizo logic" in terms of cultural democracy reversing cultural imperialism and navigated via the new science of "Tropicology", at Instituto Nabuco in Recife, the Paulisto University School of Sociology and CEBRAP, the Brazilian Center for Analysis and Planning, in Sao Paulo, whereby true development is measured by the quality of attention the country gives to its people and its culture; it is ultimately effected by reimagining trade through restless laboratory-based experimentation with institutions, ideas and techniques coupled with the ability to question and revise our shared institutional and imaginative assumptions.*

We now turn to our Epilogue for a means of accrediting Innovation Driven Institutionalized Research.

References

Burke, P. and Pallares-Burke, M. (2006) *Gilberto Freyre: Social Theory in the Tropics*. Witney, Oxfordshire: Peter Lang.

Cardoso, F. (2001) *Charting a New Course: The Politic of Globalization and Social Transformation*. New York: Rowman & Littlefield.

Cardoso, F. (1992) *Dependency and Development in Latin America*. Berkeley, CA: University of California Press.

De Onis, J. (1992) *The Green Cathedral: Sustainable Development of Amazonia*. Oxford: Oxford University Press.

Freyre, G. (1974) *The Gilbert Freyre Reader*. New York: Random House.

Hildebrandt, Z. (2001) *Marina Silva: Defending Rainforest Communities in Brazil*. New York: Feminist Press of City University.

Lessem, R. (2015) *Integral Advantage: Revisiting Emerging Markets and Societies*. Abingdon: Routledge.

Mangabeira Unger, R. (2004) *False Necessity: Anti-Necessarian Social Theory in the Service of Radical Democracy*. London: Verso.

Mangabeira Unger, R. (2014) *The Future of Religion*. Cambridge, MA: Harvard University Press.

O'Neil, J. (2011) *The Growth Map: Economic Opportunity in the BRICS and Beyond*. London: Penguin.

Epilogue
Accrediting innovation driven institutionalized research

The alternative route maps, so to speak, set out below, from Community activation (from my previous volume, *Community Activation for Integral Development*) to Awakening integral consciousness and now onto most specifically *Innovation Driven Institutionalised Research*, all featured here, constitute the three respective, alternative paths – "southern" *relational*, "eastern" *renewal* and "north-western" green *reasoned realisation* – that enable you to assess/accredit your pursuit of CARE, most especially institutionally but also individually. What is very important, moreover, to bear in mind, is that such a pursuit of CARE, individually and collectively, is not simple, a linear and sequential process. Elements of Community activation will continue, GENE-tically throughout your Awakening of integral consciousness, and then onto *innovation driven Research* and the *Embodiment of integral development* (see prospective volume to follow). Rome, or overall CARE, was not built in a day, or even in a decade!

ReLational Communal activation GENE

Fulfil livelihoods (G), establish permaculture (E), participatory research (N), marketing to community building (E)

Relational communal grounding and origination:
fulfilling livelihoods

1 underpinned by ubuntu ("I am because you are");
2 you add natural and communal value;
3 you build up social capital organizationally and/or communally;
4 culminating in communal/organizational common ownership.

*Relational emergent communal foundation: establishing
permaculture*

1   you pursue earth justice, balancing "wild" and "natural" law;
2   healing the earth through eco-economic exchange;
3   you also build cultural, social and economic worth organizationally/
societally;
4   participating communally/organizationally in the great work of nature.

*Emancipatory relational navigation: participatory
action research*

1   you recognize a community's life world (*vivencia*);
2   enhancing such via people's self development organizationally/societally;
3   reinforced via action research, in alternating action and reflection
cycles;
4   you consolidate on this by continuously animating the whole community.

Transformative relational effect: marketing to community building

1   via socio-economic exchange you provide a value base to a community;
2   build on community/organizational culture via justice and reconciliation;
3   social business becomes the means of micro or macro navigation for
you;
4   making a powerful effect through work or community-based democracy.

ReLational Awakening of integral consciousness GENE

Integrative humanism (G), southern world (E), relational research (N), people economics (E)

Relational grounding of integral awakening: integrative humanism

1   you tap into the cultural/spiritual sources of your organization/society;
2   harness and synthesize strengths to obviate weaknesses;
3   you adopt laws of integrativity (A and B both true), and complementarity;
4   bring about a massive web of reality via different scientific traditions.

Relational awakening: emergent foundation – southern world

1   you incorporate integral realities – diverse worldviews of people/
communities;
2   releasing integral rhythms – out of local identity towards global integrity;

3   identify integral <u>realms</u> – <u>nature, culture, technology, economy, polity;</u>
4   draw initially on integral <u>rounds</u> – <u>self, community, organization, society.</u>

Relational awakening: emancipate and navigate – relational
research

1   you begin especially with <u>descriptive</u> research <u>method/origination;</u>
2   you move prospectively to <u>phenomenological</u> research <u>methodology/</u>
    <u>foundation;</u>
3   you penultimately focus in particular on <u>feminist critique/emancipation;</u>
4   culminating over time with <u>participatory action research/transformation.</u>

Relational awakening: transformative effect – people economics

1   <u>work</u> you ultimately create <u>is a livelihood</u> for individuals providing for
    their needs;
2   such <u>work</u> provides a context <u>to actualize your</u>/their greatest <u>potential;</u>
3   this <u>work is a focus for cooperation</u> continually between yourselves;
4   <u>work provides</u> ultimately necessary and <u>useful goods for your people</u>
    and society.

ReLationally Innovation Driven Institutionalized Research GENE

Constitute the South (G), communiversity (E), social research
paradigm (N), social economy (E)

Relational research grounding and origination: constitute the South

1   you anthropologically <u>constitute original democracy;</u>
2   your interactive Linkages in <u>temporary federations continually reform;</u>
3   <u>you evolve male and female age sets</u> as social, economic and political
    systems;
4   <u>through cooperatively self-governing</u> mutual consensus.

Emergent emancipatory relational research: <u>Communiversity</u>

1   *Pax natura* underlies nature and community and is thereby local;
2   *Pax spiritus* underlies culture and spirituality as a Pax Africana-based
    sanctuary;
3   *Pax scientia* underlies science and technology and thereby a research
    academy;
4   *Pax economica* underlies economy and enterprise, as a social laboratory.

Relation research emergent foundation: social research paradigm

1   you pursue a quest for social innovation, via a relational orientation;
2   uncovering why social innovation lags behind technological innovation;
3   you turn individual, analytic method into societally transformative methodology;
4   you collectively find a way to institutionalize social research and innovation.

Relational institutional research effect: social economy

1   grounded in sovereignty of labour and subordinate nature of capital;
2   via cooperation between academy, laboratory, enterprise;
3   navigating via participatory management, personalism, cooperativism;
4   ultimately effecting your/their cooperatively based social economy.

ReNewing Communal activation GENE

Communiversity (G), vitality of place (E), study circles (N), social business (E)

Grounding and origination of communal renewal: Communiversity

1   your community activation is underpinned by nature power;
2   furthered through fusing tradition and modernity, prayer and work;
3   consolidated upon by combining nature, spirit, science, economy;
4   you ultimately establish a form of communitalism/communiversity within/without.

Emergent foundation of communal renewal: vitality of place

1   underpinned by your creating an underlying socio-economic value base;
2   enhanced by communal relationships, within your enterprise and/or without;
3   societally embedded in the vitality of your particular place;
4   resulting in trade and accumulation both micro and macro in nature.

Emancipatory navigation of communal renewal: study circles

1   you renew genuine interest in individual and collective learning;
2   enhanced by the informal character of your study circles;

3   navigated via a <u>flexible framework to support learning</u> and development;
4   resulting in collective <u>learning, of/through self, community, organization.</u>

Transformed effect of communal renewal: <u>social business</u>

1   you begin by creating <u>community to provide the economic value base;</u>
2   you individually and collectively <u>start the economic engine at the rear;</u>
3   building up towards <u>creating a micro world without poverty;</u>
4   such community building results in the <u>proliferation of social business.</u>

ReNewed <u>A</u>wakening of integral consciousness GENE

Consciousness spectrum (G), innovation ecosystem (E), institutional ecology (N), HR to conscious evolution (E)

Ground conscious renewal: consciousness spectrum

1   newly evoking the <u>ancient Indian chakra energy spectrum;</u>
2   altogether providing an <u>antidote to the clash of cultures;</u>
3   <u>as a spectrum of consciousness</u> and integration, individually and organizationally;
4   <u>turning creative vision into total quality</u> management.

Awaken renewal: emergent foundation – innovation ecosystem

1   grounding and origination of consciousness,<u> local identity, stewardship</u>;
2   an emergent foundation as a <u>local–global "non-entity" – catalyzation;</u>
3   co-evolve <u>newly global</u> emancipatory navigational <u>entity – research;</u>
4   ultimate transformative effect leads onto <u>global integrity – facilitation.</u>

Awaken renewal: navigate emancipation – institutional ecology

1   <u>ground – activate</u> community through a <u>communal learning</u> initiative;
2   <u>emerge – awaken</u> cognitive, affective, behavioural, value-laden <u>awareness;</u>
3   <u>navigate – research academy</u> in economic, educational, communal sectors;
4   <u>effect – embodying sustainable development</u>, socio-technical laboratory.

Awaken renewal: transformative effect – conscious evolution

1   <u>grounding in spiritual consciousness</u> not in labour as a commodity;
2   emerging though a <u>co-evolved knowledge-based </u>evolutionary spiral;

3   co-navigating <u>via a conscious organization</u> based on a full spectrum;
4   <u>effected through conscious evolution via Japanese-style kyosei/co-evolution</u>.

ReNewed Innovation Driven Institutionalized Research GENE

Commonwealth (G), social ecology (E), integral academy (N), operations to knowledge creation (E)

Grounding and origination of research renewal: commonwealth

1   your research is <u>embodied in</u> spiritualized religion via a <u>commonwealth</u>;
2   furthered through <u>a marriage between different worlds;</u>
3   natural, economic, cultural and social systems <u>lodged in spiritual science;</u>
4   whereby you <u>reclaim the land and renew enterprise</u>/community/society.

Renewed foundation of institutionalized research: social ecology

1   you replace "I am because I have power" with "I am because we are";
2   emerging via spirit, rhythm and creativity set within our GENE;
3   navigating new meaning, motif, ethos, mode, function, method and form;
4   effecting a social ecology – leadership, knowledge and industry ecology.

Emancipatory navigation of institutional research: integral academy

1   a <u>community academy</u> serves to institutionalize community activation;
2   a <u>developmental academy</u> serves to awaken individual/group consciousness;
3   a <u>research academy</u> underlies innovation driven, institutionalized research;
4   an <u>academy of life</u> is one where transformative education takes place.

Transformed effect of institutionalized research: knowledge creation

1   you ground origination in a <u>knowledge and value base;</u>
2   emerging <u>middle–up–down–across</u> through a <u>knowledge crew;</u>
3   you navigate via a <u>hierarchical business or academic functional system;</u>
4   you effect via a <u>networked</u>, autonomous, interdependent <u>project layer</u>.

ReaSoned realization of Communal activation GENE

Self-government (G), disclose new worlds (E), wealth of networks (N), mutual advantage (E)

Grounding/origination of communal realization: self-government

1   you engage in direct democracy;
2   evolving through the evocation of a big restorative picture;
3   amplified by a discursive community;
4   effected via individual and group individuation to actualize a truth quest.

Emergent foundation of reasoned realisation: disclose new worlds

1   you exhibit/encourage virtuous citizenship in your enterprise or without;
2   enhanced by cultivating solidarity in your enterprise and/or community;
3   consolidated by disclosing altogether new worlds within or without;
4   altogether engaging in social, cultural or economic history making.

Emancipatory navigation of reason-realization: wealth of networks

1   you provide commons laden purpose to your community/organization;
2   enhanced through peer-to-peer relationships in such;
3   building socially and technologically through open source connectivity;
4   results in community based and institutionalized research networks.

Transformed effect of reasoned realization: mutual advantage

1   soil, river, forest provide the value and research base;
2   you become purveyors of your region as institutional researchers;
3   build on such through a provincial diversity of socio-economic structures;
4   effect via powerful cultural, political, economic local government (*zemtsvo*).

ReaSoned realization of Awakened integral consciousness GENE

Integral theory (G), spiral integral (E), integral innovation (N), integral awakening (N)

Awakening reason: grounding/origination – integral theory

1   Wilber's 4 Quadrants – intentional, behavioural, socio-technical, cultural;
2   all Quadrants/all levels – egocentric, ethnocentric, world/centric;

3   multiple intelligences – logical, verbal, spatial, interpersonal, intrapersonal;
4   subject to States and Types – gross, subtle, causal, and masculine/feminine.

Awakening reason: emergent foundation – spiral integral

1   alternate between individual expressive and collective sacrificial;
2   accommodating a double helix – memetic structure and prevailing conditions;
3   you emerge in two tiers – survival to egalitarian, flex/flow to holonomic;
4   your culminating effect is to promote human (self/societal) emergence.

Awakening reason: emancipatory navigation – integral innovation – TIPS

1   you focus on People – managing self and others;
2   you systemically manage interdependence and complexity – Systems;
3   you promote Innovation – "Mode 2" production of new knowledge;
4   resulting in social and/or material technologies.

Awakening reason: transformative effect – integral awakening

1   uncover soil, soul, society relating to nature, self and social relationships;
2   reveal earth democracy to understand ourselves as planetary beings;
3   realize knowledge society for sustained and inclusive growth;
4   as Sarvodaya herald the integral awakening of all – self, community, world.

ReaSoned realization of Innovation Driven Research GENE

Truth–goodness–beauty (G), integral development (E),
reinvent knowledge (N), solidary economy (E)

Grounding reasoned institutional research: truth, goodness, beauty

1   institutionalized research is grounded in truth, goodness and beauty;
2   emerge through scientific, managerial and artistic creativity;
3   navigated via phases of creativity, elaboration and orientation;
4   effected by innovators – entrepreneurial, scientific and artistic.

Emergent reasoned institutional research: integral development

1   centred in community – co-creating ecosystems, community activation;
2   culture – renew self, organization and society; awakening consciousness;

3 innovation – <u>regenerating knowledge</u>, institutionalized research;
4 impact – <u>social innovation</u>, actualizing development.

Emancipatory navigation of reasoned research: reinvent knowledge

1 conceive of an <u>integrated genealogy</u> rather than a standardized university;
2 research aligned with <u>community, sanctuary, academy, laboratory;</u>
3 connecting and renewing <u>oral, scriptural, textual and digital forms;</u>
4 interactive laboratory <u>releasing GENE-ius</u>/recognizing GENEalogy.

Transformative effect of reasoned research: solidary economy

1 institutionalized research <u>grounded in rainforest eco-services;</u>
2 via "<u>mestizo logic</u>" – <u>cultural democracy</u> reverses cultural imperialism;
3 development measured by <u>quality of attention given to people/culture;</u>
4 effect by <u>reimagining trade experimenting with ideas/institutions.</u>

Index

For Product Safety Concerns and Information please contact our EU
representative GPSR@taylorandfrancis.com
Taylor & Francis Verlag GmbH, Kaufingerstraße 24, 80331 München, Germany

www.ingramcontent.com/pod-product-compliance
Ingram Content Group UK Ltd.
Pitfield, Milton Keynes, MK11 3LW, UK
UKHW021838240425
457818UK00007B/223